MW01042103

# Superhighway to Wealth

## Making Money on the Net

Lee & Kristy Phillips

**Superhighway to Wealth**
by Lee & Kristy Phillips



Second Edition
Printed in the United States of America

Information Directions, Ltd.
470 North University Ave. #203
Provo, UT 84601

e-mail: ksp@infodirect.com



ISBN 0-9649424-1-0

# Contents

## Section III - The Internet Market Place



## Section IV - Internet Business Checklist

# Introduction

Colonizing the new world, the land rush, the gold rush, the space race, and the computer revolution each presented unique opportunities for people to find their fortune. Many people took advantage of the opportunities when they presented themselves and became very rich, but nothing in history can compare to the wealth and freedom available on the Information Superhighway. It now presents the single most significant opportunity to stake a claim and make a fortune that has ever been presented. The opportunity the Information Superhighway offers is unprecedented because you can seek your fortune without taking big risks or even leaving your home.

The Information Superhighway not only presents opportunities for individuals, it also presents businesses with huge opportunities to make profits. The business and financial worlds are in the midst of a revolution that is changing the world — your world. Barriers of time and distance, barriers that have cost businesses millions of dollars to span in the past, are disappearing. This revolution is being led by the amazing advances in computer technology and the explosive growth of information.

Today, the Information Superhighway is basically synonymous with the global network of computers called the "Internet," or just the "Net." This global network of networks links millions of people throughout the world like a giant invisible spider web crisscrossing the globe. The Internet may be the most powerful communication resource ever created. It transports huge quantities of information every second. It may soon prove to be the most effective marketing tool ever created. It is the union of knowledge and technology, and it gives anyone who knows how to use it a big competitive advantage over those who don't.

Countries, businesses, individuals—everyone expends their energies trying to obtain a power advantage over their competitors. Albert Einstein's name is a household word because he gave the Allies power over their adversaries in World War II when his theories led to production of the atomic bomb. His formula, $E=MC^2$, is now a fundamental part of physics. This equation says that Energy is equal to Mass multiplied by the speed of light (C) squared. Today, there is an equation that will give the business world as much power as Einstein's equation gave the scientific world—P=KC.

Simply put, P=KC means Power equals Knowledge times the speed of light. "Knowledge is Power" may seem trite, but most people will agree that it is true. What the world has yet to realize fully is that the Information Superhighway, the Internet, can bring you the world's knowledge, neatly organized in your home or office computer, and it can bring you all of this knowledge literally at the speed of light. That means that a letter, report, picture, or any other form of information can be transmitted from any point on earth in seconds.

When you can access knowledge, the world's knowledge, at the speed of light, the amount of power that you can control is almost inconceivable. How much knowledge is available? Information from state and national governments, schools, libraries, businesses, and individuals from all over the world can be accessed in minutes. That information can be in the form of text, pictures, even video clips—anything that can be put into a computer. In a real sense, you can bring an unlimited amount of information instantly into your home or office.

There is an important corollary, or second formula, to the equation P=KC, and that is P=W, or Power equals Wealth. When power is used to maximize commerce and business, it is easily converted to wealth. The age of electronic commerce is now waiting to be capitalized, either by you or by others. It's beginning now, and what happens on the Internet in the next few years will have a greater impact on your life than the computer has had. Your life will be dramatically changed by the Internet, whether you like it or not.

We are truly on the brink of an electronic era that is changing the world. Think back at how new technologies have affected people. When the printing press was invented, the elite—the rich—passed laws that prevented the public from accessing this new technology called books. They knew that if they could keep the knowledge to themselves, they could control wealth and maintain their power. As a result, it took hundreds of years before nearly everyone could read, and when the masses could read, the wealth of society became more evenly distributed. Similarly, for decades only the rich and powerful had automobiles. For thirty years, the telephone was a tool of the elite. The television took less than twenty years to become a household fixture.

Computers and computer technology used to be considered mysterious tools of the elite, the rich, and the powerful. Only ten years ago, many people thought that they didn't need to learn how to use a computer; they could leave that for the next generation. Some of them believed that only smart, special people could use or could even learn how to use the computer, and they became afraid of it. Today, the fact is, you probably use a computer at work, at the library, to get money from your bank account, or do countless other things. If you work in an office, you almost certainly have to know how to do word processing on a computer. Students graduating from high schools and colleges are required to be computer literate. If you don't already use a computer proficiently, don't let computers scare you! You don't have to know everything about computers to use one. Do you have to know about the inner workings of a telephone to make a call? Do you have to be able to fix an internal combustion engine to drive a car? Of course not. And, you can use your computer to access the Internet without knowing much about computers.

> *If you can point and click,*
> *you can use the Internet.*
> *It's Easy!*

Computers are becoming easier to use because the software programs that make the computer respond to commands are becoming more sophisticated and "user friendly." Software such as Netscape Navigator, Mosaic, and Internet Explorer make the Internet very easy to use. One of the more recent software developments has been made by Synthonics Technologies, Inc. Their software allows anyone to put objects easily into a 3-D format for viewing and manipulation in a computer. The graphics can be viewed in full 3-D stereo vision without expensive headsets, liquid crystal glasses, or Polaroid glasses, and the other cumbersome devices commonly found in 3-D viewing. Their software also makes it "point and click" easy to interact with 3-D objects on the Net. The objects can be turned, moved, opened, shut, or manipulated in any way appropriate.

The fast-paced and ever-changing world of the Internet undergoes constant, exciting evolution. New programming languages such as Java and Shockwave allow programmers to create animated graphics for Web sites. The growing capabilities for adding voice messages to e-mail, and Synthonics' 3-D Maker, which creates true walk-around 3-D graphics, are just a few of the amazing developments that are making the Net a world of its own. Furthermore, companies such as Netscape and Microsoft are devising ways to make these enhancements easy for anyone to use. If you want to be part of the Internet frontier, get involved now.

The computer has changed our lives for the better and made more people millionaires than any prior technology. In the days before everyone started to use the computer, some ordinary people, people just like you and me, saw its potential. In just a few years, Bill Gates, an obscure college student, became the richest man in America and built the same type of fortune it took the Fords, Rockefellers, and Kennedys generations to build.

Today physical and financial survival are increasingly dependent on utilizing cutting edge technology. Gates states that the fortunes made on the Internet may surpass his, and that they will be made even faster by people that have never been heard of today. Why shouldn't that be you? All you have to do is understand how to use the Internet and have a good idea. You cannot afford to delay. Technology development is moving faster and faster with each new invention. The people who saw the potential of computers had only one decade to capitalize on its power before everyone had access to the computer. Currently only a small percentage of North Americans have had an experience on the Internet, but it is predicted that the Internet will be in nearly every home by the year 2003. If you can see the power of the Internet, the time to make your move is now. You have to be quick to take advantage of the opportunities presented by new technologies such as the Internet. Those who hesitate really will be lost.

# Section I

# Internet Background

# Chapter 1

## What is Cyberspace?

The Internet is the fastest growing, most amazing communication medium on the planet. The Internet ties the world's computers together creating exciting new horizons for users. There are currently millions of computers hooked together from almost 200 countries around the world. The users of these computers communicate, work, play, and travel in the place known as "cyberspace."

What is cyberspace? Where is cyberspace? Cyberspace is the place that everyone hears about, but most are hard pressed to define. It is the shadowy space where computer data exist and communication takes place. Think of cyberspace as a computer-generated neighborhood that exists without the physical liabilities of reality. As in any neighborhood, there are libraries, stores, theaters—everything you can imagine. Anyone can visit and work there, not physically, but virtually.

To understand where cyberspace exists, imagine the place your voice is when you are talking on the telephone. This is a good place to start, because the telephone system is the basic connection or gateway that lets you enter cyberspace. The wires and cables of the telephone system are the roads, the transportation system in cyberspace, but they make up only a part of cyberspace. Now, imagine the area where bytes and bits of data "live" in your computer. Here the cities of cyberspace exist with millions and billions of resident ideas, thoughts, conversations, and views. Multiply these images to include the millions of computers hooked together by the Internet. Finally, imagine how the data create the virtual neighborhood of real people interacting in an imaginary world that can be visited anytime from anywhere on earth. Combine all of these images, and the place that results is cyberspace, also known as the Net, the Web, and the Information Superhighway. Cyberspace is a world of virtual reality.

In the virtual world of cyberspace, being connected to the Internet is being connected to the world and its information. Entering cyberspace removes all physical barriers. You can travel, find information, make contact with people, and do things that would be physically impossible to do in any other way. All cyberspace contacts and activities are experienced virtually. For instance, you can visit the White House and hand messages to the President. The contact is real, but there are none of the physical restraints commonly associated with visiting the White House. You don't have to fly to Washington, D.C. or pay for a hotel. The President doesn't worry about security. While at the White House, you can order copies of the

President's speeches, and they will be handed to you instantly, just as if you were *actually* standing there. It sounds incredible, but it is real, or at least it is virtually real.

This virtual reality gives the Internet a sense of community—a global community of people who share a wide variety of resources. In this book, citizens of this community, i.e., people who use the Internet, will be called "netters." Netters share thoughts, ideas, joy, pain, and other aspects of life. They consider the people they meet in cyberspace as friends; sometimes even romances develop. One gentleman became acquainted with "the woman of his life" online and "married the lovely lady." She lived in California; he lived on the eastern seaboard. Now they have a home and family in Vermont. Thousands of people are meeting on the Internet each day, and some become lifelong companions.

You may have read newspaper stories that demonstrate just how closely-knit netters are. One example is the story of a group of senior citizens who communicated every morning with each other over the Internet. One morning it was obvious that one lady was not communicating clearly. She didn't say she was having problems, but she just wasn't normal in the "eyes" of the other netters who knew her well. The netters notified the paramedics in her city, and an ambulance was immediately sent to the lady's address. The netters are now credited with saving her life.

The Internet community is unique. It extends beyond anything the world has ever known, and it may be one of the major instruments that brings peace to the world. On the Net people only see your mind with its wit, humor, brilliance, and eloquence or its lack thereof. You have the chance to present yourself in your true spirit, whatever your spirit is.

The Internet removes physical barriers that restrict people in the real world. A veteran from Florida explains: "I'm a disabled vet. I used to have three choices—I could stare at three walls, I could watch TV, or I could go to bed. That's dying." When he found the Internet, he had a fourth option, and it has made all the difference in his life.

Cyberspace fills many needs for netters who frequent its domain, but there are still some things that a face-to-face meeting can accomplish that can't be done in cyberspace. As more and more people recognize what the Internet can do for them and see the wealth of resources offered along the Information Superhighway, its highways will be expanded. Every day netters think of new, exciting ways to use the Internet. The Internet is not just a fad. It is not a passing high tech toy that netters have formed a little club to play with. The Internet is the most powerful communication tool ever created. The development and use of the Internet may prove to be a pivotal point in human civilization, especially in business and education.

How can these statements be made? After all, an editorial comment recently made on one of the United States' most powerful radio stations stated that the Internet would soon disappear and would go down in history as a fad. Not so!

When computers were first introduced, many people dismissed them as a fad, too. But the computer is definitely not a fad. Until now your personal computer has basically been used as a family typewriter or toy. You actually played games on your computer. You used it to keep track of numbers on spreadsheets, write letters, and to draw pictures. Your computer never gave you anything you didn't put into it. You had to buy a computer program and load it into your computer or you physically typed, or possibly scanned, information into your computer. The Internet now allows your computer to go out and retrieve information—literally the world's information—and bring it back to you at the speed of light.

Right now there is an infinite array of text, files, bulletins, reference sources, statistics, electronic journals, research reports, government information, and more, waiting for you in cyberspace. So much wealth exists that most people can't grasp its magnitude and value. Those who quickly learn to use the Internet as something more than a high tech toy will harness its wealth and find incredible power. The Information Superhighway welcomes adventurous entrepreneurs who recognize and want to apply its resources to expand businesses in the real world. Clearly a new era of business on the Internet is underway, but it is still in its infancy. How to effectively turn the wealth of cyberspace into real wealth in the real world is the challenge that awaits each businessperson who is ready to venture into the world of cyberspace.

# Chapter 2

## History

It seems as if everyone is talking about the Internet and how to use it. Everyone thinks it is an exciting, new concept. It certainly is exciting, but the Internet is not new. In one form or another, the Internet has been around since the late sixties. However, the general population is just now becoming aware of it. The Net is being publicized in a growing number of talk shows, newspapers, magazines, and even movies. The table on the next page shows the number of times the words "Internet," "Information Superhighway," and "World Wide Web" were used in articles published between 1989 and 1996. (The World Wide Web is a fast growing feature of the Internet which is becoming so popular that some netters are beginning to refer to the Internet as the "World Wide Web" or "the Web.")

Where did the Internet come from? The idea of a national network of computers was first conceived of and implemented by the military. The military's first national network was called ARPAnet (Advanced Research Projects

| KEY WORD SEARCH | | | | |
|---|---|---|---|---|
| Year | Internet | Information Superhighway | Internet & Information Superhighway | World Wide Web |
| 1990 | 1,540 | 16 | 4 | * |
| 1991 | 2,994 | 87 | 16 | * |
| 1992 | 4,671 | 98 | 13 | * |
| 1993 | 9,085 | 2,970 | 356 | * |
| 1994 | 32,295 | 18,198 | 4,125 | 3,318 |
| 1995 | 124,666 | 14,130 | 6,849 | 42,149 |
| 1996 | 314,221 | 8,452 | 5,621 | 98,293 |

* The World Wide Web was not widely available until 1993.

Agency network). ARPAnet was originally an experimental network of computers designed to support military research and to protect information that might be destroyed in bomb attacks or natural disasters. The network had to continue to function even if one of the computer sites were compromised. To achieve this goal, the designers had to assume that any part of the network could be destroyed at any moment. To overcome this problem, the developers made it possible for every computer on the network to "talk" to every other computer. The computers communicated with a special computer message exchange or "protocol" that each computer on the network used. As part of the "protocol," each computer was programmed to send any message it received on to "adjoining" computers until the message was finally received at the designated location. If, for some reason, one computer could not contact a specific adjoining computer, it could contact one of the other computers on the network and reroute the message. This process, called dynamic rerouting, ensured that communication would be accomplished even if one or more of the computers in the network were not functioning.

The original military "protocol" allowed all of the computers on the Internet to "talk" to each other. It was designed so that every message sent over the network was divided into a series of separate envelopes or "Internet protocol packets." This same protocol is still used today. When a message is sent over the Internet, each packet is addressed and sent individually as an Internet protocol packet to the proper computer destination. The packets are sent out at separate times, and they may not each take the same route as they travel though the Internet. For instance, a message sent from San Diego, California to Washington, D.C. might be divided into two or three separate packets. One packet could go from San Diego to Salt Lake City to Chicago and finally arrive in Washington. Another packet could route through Denver, Atlanta, Miami, Richmond, and then to Washington. The route each packet takes doesn't matter because the computer in Washington will receive the various packets and assemble them in the proper order, so that the receiver can read the message. Some of the packets may actually travel around the world. The packets are numbered, and if one of the packets is damaged or lost in transit, the receiving computer will send for another identical packet. The whole process takes place at the speed of light. To netters observing the process, everything is done almost instantly.

Although there was only one network with four computers when ARPAnet began, the military "protocol" that was developed was designed to allow tens of thousands of networks and computers to communicate and work together using the telephone lines. The protocol may seem obvious today, but when it was first developed, it was a farsighted strategy. In an inspiring spirit of cooperation, computer programmers and scientists around the world were able to agree on a protocol that is now used in every country on every computer hooked to the Internet.

During the Gulf War in 1991, the U.S. found out just how effective the ARPAnet protocol model really was. The American military had considerable trouble knocking out the Iraqi command network. It turned out that the Iraqis were using an antiquated commercially available network with the standard Internet protocol and its routing and recovery technology. Even the early versions of the dynamic rerouting system really worked. The U.S. military was perturbed that the Iraqi system was hard to destroy, but was elated to think of advantages their advanced system gave them.

About ten years after ARPAnet was created, Local Area Networks (LANs) began to appear. LANs are a series of computers physically connected by some type of dedicated cable. The computers connected to a LAN system are usually located in the same office or company facility, and the cable is just strung from computer to computer. When several LANs are connected by special cables, the system is called a Wide Area Network (WAN). It is cost prohibitive for most companies to string cables between two remote locations in order to form WANs.

In the 1970's, the military contractors and universities that did research for the military and had LAN networks wanted to connect with ARPAnet rather than go to the expense of making WANs. It was obvious that if all of the LANs could communicate with each other, everyone doing work for the military would benefit.

One of the most important early WANs was the NSFNET run by the National Science Foundation (NSF), an agency of the United States Government. Originally the NSF also planned to use ARPAnet for communication, but this strategy failed due to bureaucracy and staffing problems.

It was necessary for the NSF to build its own Wide Area Network. They decided to use the same protocol created for ARPAnet. The creators of NSFNET set up five supercomputer regional centers around the United States and connected the five centers together to form the "backbone" of a giant WAN. The NSF planned to make the computing capacity in each of the five centers available to universities for scholarly research. Only five centers were created because each center was so expensive to create and maintain.

The plan was good, but it soon became clear that if the NSF paid to connect all of the university computing centers to the main five computers on the "backbone network," it would be cost prohibitive. It was decided that each campus or research facility would be responsible to pay for its own connection and ongoing service to the closest NSF regional center. So each campus and research facility had to pay to have a cable strung between its facility and one of the five regional centers. Actually, they didn't have to pay to have a cable strung because the phone company already had cables connecting each facility with the nearest regional NSF center. All they had to do was pay the phone company for a special telephone line called a T1 line. A T1 line is nothing more than an existing telephone line configured to look and act as a dedicated cable strung between two points. The T1 line allows a tremendous amount of data to move back and forth simultaneously.

Fortunately, it soon became apparent that it wasn't necessary to string a cable or maintain a T1 line between each research center and the nearest regional NSF facility. It was sufficient to connect to the nearest university or research facility that had already connected to the NSF network. As long as each facility would "share" its connection at no cost with the next facility, the whole system would work, and connection costs would be minimal.

Cost sharing was a good solution because everyone paid for their part of the network; yet, they had the use of the entire network. It was agreed that everyone would pay for and maintain their own piece of the network in exchange for being able to use the rest of it at no additional charge. The Internet began to grow like a giant Tinker Toy.

The whole idea of maintaining your own "piece" of the network and freely sharing in everybody else's piece has grown into the worldwide network known as the Internet. This helps explain why the statement "nobody owns the Net" can be made. There is no Internet, Inc., that collects fees from all of the Internet networks and users; instead, there is worldwide cooperation. Cooperation also explains why using the Net is so inexpensive. Once you pay for your local connection, there are no other line costs—no long distance phone charges to access other computers around the world.

The early NSF "Internet" connected many universities and research facilities in the United States together. Originally the NSF planned to allow all the researchers and even the students at the universities to access the network. They believed that access would enhance research. The plan to get everyone using the network was implemented and the early NSFNET became primarily the domain of researchers and academicians, because access required knowledge of the complex computer language Unix. Today, you don't need to know anything about Unix to make good use of the Internet.

Because the early Internet was dominated by the NSF and Unix computer specialists, they defined the customs, rules, and regulations that governed use of the Internet. The NSF prohibited use of its NSFNET for any type of commercial activity. This early "Internet" was carefully and jealously controlled by the scientific elite, and it gave them a great deal of power. They never thought of the formula P=KC, but they exploited their privileged position and knew they had great power. In the early 1990's, however, a few entrepreneurs recognized the commercial value of the Internet and attempted to use it to market their products. This created tension between the academic community that wanted to maintain their control of the Internet and smart business people who wanted to take advantage of the Internet's tremendous marketing capabilities.

Now, not only has responsibility for operation of the Internet facilities changed, the rules and regulations that the early researchers and academicians established for the Net are being tested and changed as well. Although some academicians and computer specialists have wanted to continue their domination of the Internet and control its information and power, their stranglehold on the commercial use of the Internet is gone. The Internet is now open for business.

# Chapter 3

## Size and Growth

Before about 1990, when students, faculty members, and research scientists were basically the only people who had access to the Internet, the "average" netter was a male, under age 30, well educated, and had little disposable income. In the early 1990's, three important things happened which opened the Internet to the general public and the business world.

1. The World Wide Web was developed.
2. Graphical browsers made the Internet easier to use.
3. The National Science Foundation (NSF) began to allow commerce on the Internet.

### World Wide Web Developed

Although it was possible to gather information from scientists around the world, the Internet was still complicated and cumbersome to use. In order to expedite research for ongoing projects at CERN (European Laboratory for Particle Physics), consulting software engineer Tim Berners-Lee developed a system that made it possible to link documents stored on various computer systems. His goal was to make the process so easy that everyone would want to put their data on the system. Linking documents had been done on a small scale on individual personal computers (PC's); but as the Internet grew, Berners-Lee pushed for a method that would make its huge knowledge base easily accessible. In the summer of 1991 the program that he developed, the World Wide Web, was introduced on the Internet.

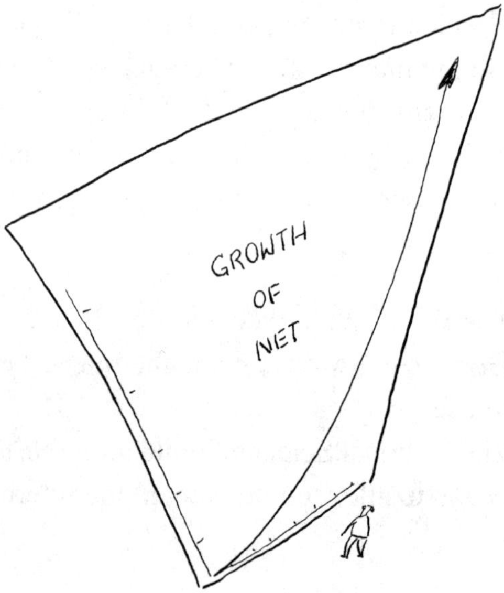


The new linking system was distinctive because each document on this global network was given a unique address, a Universal Resource Locator (URL). The document's URL identified which computer the information was stored on and established a pathway to it. It is remarkable that the world so quickly accepted and embraced this universal addressing system. (So far, the world has been unable to agree to use the metric system, the same electrical voltage, or the same television and video format.) On the Internet network, each computer has its own unique "address," just as each house in a city has a unique address. Additionally, each file of information stored has a unique address. Berners-Lee's program was designed so that addresses for information could be "randomly retrieved" over the Internet from any type of computer.

The system allowed addresses to be embedded invisibly in the text so that a netter reading the text could use the embedded addresses to jump from computer to computer exploring the information to which the embedded addresses linked them. Text that has an address behind it is called "hypertext." With the simple click of a button, hypertext allows netters to jump instantly and effortlessly from one computer to another following information prompts that interest them. The text which has an address embedded behind it is marked by underlining or by colored text. Netters know they can obtain more information on the topic described by the marked text by clicking their mouse button on it. With a simple click, they activate the embedded address.

The World Wide Web, or simply the "Web," uses hypertext linking to tie the computers on the Internet together. Of course, in order to be accessible using Web programs, the information must be stored in the computer using the Web or hypertext storage format, and it must be given a Web address. There are massive amounts of information available on the Internet which are not stored in Web format, but more and more information is being filed away in computers around the world so that it is accessible using World Wide Web compatible programs.

Berners-Lee's program, combined with the powerful searching programs that are now used on the Internet, makes it possible for anyone to use the Internet and find lots of information on whatever they want. A little bit of training may be necessary, but there is absolutely no requirement that netters know anything about complex computer programs.

## Graphical Browsers Created

The creation of graphical browsers made the Internet easier to use and more accessible to everyone. In order to read documents stored in hypertext format, a netter needs to use a browser. The browser is a computer program which reads and displays hypertext documents. Just as you wouldn't be able to compose documents on your computer without a word processor, hypertext documents are not easily retrieved without a browser.

In 1992, Marc Andreesen, a 21-year old student at the University of Illinois, and his friend and programming wizard, Eric Bina, created Mosaic. Mosaic is an easy-to-use graphical "Web browser" that uses hypertext links, or "hyperlinks," to connect hypertext documents in a point and click environment. Mosaic made it possible to easily locate and view not only text, but pictures and other graphics on the Internet. Mosaic moved the world of the Web into the world of graphics and sound. Hyperlinks could suddenly transport sound and even videos over the Internet. The World Wide Web portion of the Internet became an exciting place to visit for the visual and sound effects in addition to the information that could be found there.

To understand how to use Mosaic, picture a sentence typed on your computer screen with a word or phrase which is highlighted in some way. For example, the word will be written in blue letters while the rest of the text is written in black letters. This highlighted phrase or word is the information or "flag" that has a hyperlink address invisibly hidden behind it. When the cursor is moved over the hypertext, the cursor arrow shape changes to the shape of a hand. By simply clicking on the highlighted word, the hidden address is "activated," and the information stored at the location designated by the hidden address is then displayed. With Mosaic, movement on the Internet can be accomplished by the click of a button.

As soon as it was made available, Mosaic was a success. Finally, it was possible for anyone to move around the Net and access text and graphics without being a computer whiz. By November, 1993, other computer experts at the National Center for Super-computing Applications (NCSA), where Andreesen and Bina worked, had written mass applications for Mosaic in Windows and Macintosh formats, which made Mosaic available to every computer user.

When Mosaic was introduced in the spring of 1993, Internet growth exploded. Statistics compiled by Merit,

Inc., indicate that in 1993, traffic on the World Wide Web was measured at 443,931% the amount of the previous year; in 1994 the growth was 1713%. Even Gopher traffic showed a remarkable increase of over 1000% in 1993 and almost 200% in 1994. (Gopher is an older Internet program used to search for information on the Internet.) In 1993, Internet users who advertised over the Internet more than doubled in number from 19,664 to 42,883.

After graduation from the University of Illinois, Andreesen moved to "Silicon Valley" south of San Francisco and eventually teamed up with Jim Clark, founder of Silicon Graphics. They formed the company Netscape and created what they called a "Mosaic-killer." Netscape Navigator came out in late 1994 and was an even bigger hit than Mosaic, almost immediately claiming 70% of the browser market. On August 9, 1995, Netscape gave the public its first opportunity to buy stock in its company. What happened that day is fast becoming legend. The opening price was $28. Within minutes it had soared to $\$74\frac{3}{4}$. By the end of the day it had settled at $58, making the company worth more than $2 billion and its founders instant multi-millionaires.

## NSF Allowed Commercial Use of the Internet

In the early 1990's, the National Science Foundation redefined its view that the Net was only to be used for science and research. They recognized that business on the Internet could be very useful, and that the Internet could become a very powerful business tool. The National

Science Foundation decided to lift the ban on the commercial sector, and business began to be done on the Internet. Of course, the Internet still remains a powerful research tool, but the "official" ban on commerce over the Net has been completely removed.

But, change takes time. So unfortunately, some of the scientific users continued to chastise people who did business on the Net, but their efforts to keep business off the Internet were overwhelmed by the sheer volume of business that was being done. When someone is severely chastised over the Internet they have been "flamed."

Once the NSF lifted its ban on commercial use of the Internet and the Internet became available to the public, companies called "local access providers" or "Internet Service Providers" (ISPs) began to spring up around the country. ISPs maintain special computer equipment and high-bandwidth phone lines to "tap" into the Internet. The ISPs "sublet" their equipment and phone lines to end-users like you. You use their service to access the Internet. Your computer uses a modem to "call" the ISP you are working with, and their equipment "patches" you directly into the Internet. If you're going to spend much time at all on the

Net, accessing the Internet using an ISP is usually much cheaper than accessing it through an "online service" such as AOL, CompuServe, or the Microsoft Network.

On April 30, 1995, the National Science Foundation effectively bowed out of the Internet business and transferred most of its Internet backbone facilities to a group of commercial entities. The main junctions of the commercial Internet are connection points called NAPs (Network Access Points). There are four "Network Access Points." The commercial companies Ameritech, PacBell, Sprint, and MFS Datanet are each responsible for maintaining one of the Network Access Points. However, these companies do not own or regulate the Net; they only maintain and provide the basic backbone structure for the massive worldwide area network everyone calls the Internet. The very high speed backbone network services are still funded by the NSF, even though they are maintained and serviced by private companies.

## Demographics

Since these three developments occurred, the growth in the number of Internet users has been nothing short of astounding. A Nielsen Media Research survey conducted for CommerceNet in 1995 shows that there are over 37 million people with access to the Internet in the U.S. and Canada alone. The Internet is now accessible in almost 200 countries, and the International Data Group sets the number of Internet users at 89 million worldwide.

As more and more people connect to the Internet, the picture of the "average" Internet user is changing.

According to the Nielsen survey, the percentage of professionals and managerial people using the World Wide Web, the fastest growing part of the Internet, has risen to 50% of the total number of users.

> *The average Internet user . . .*
> ← *is educated*
> ← *is progressive*
> ← *has money to spend*

One-fourth of Web users have an income over $80,000 a year (compared to 10% in the general population), and 64% have a college degree (compared to 28% in the general population). Today's Internet users are well-educated, progressive and have money to spend. Two-thirds of Internet users access the Internet from work, and nearly 40% of the users have access in their homes. Only 8% of the respondents are now accessing the Internet from a school or university. The days when the Internet was dominated by scientists and academicians are gone. Obviously, many businesses are starting to use the Internet, and people with vision are realizing what the Internet can do for them both personally and professionally.

In the future, what will the average Internet travelers be like? They will be male, female, children, teens, and adults. They will be Fortune 500 companies, small entrepreneurs, students, senior citizens, doctors, dietitians, lawyers, and librarians. The Internet remains an invaluable tool for research and communication. It is now also an invaluable tool for business.

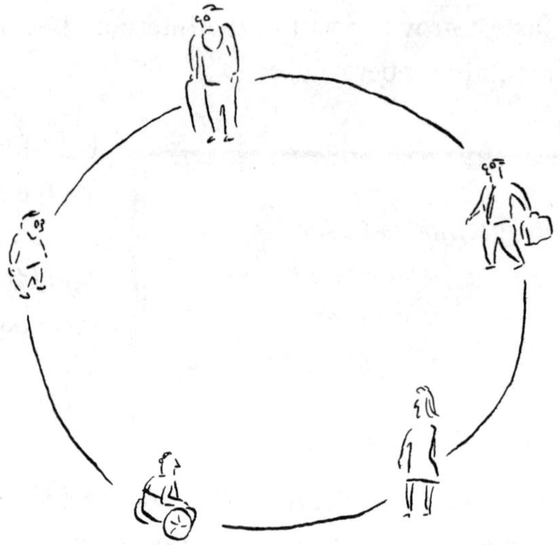

Electronic shopping for both products and services is going to increase tremendously as more and more people discover the convenience and value of using the Internet. You can order everything from groceries to legal advice, and fancy chocolates to complete electronic books on the Internet. You can find a translator for your overseas business dealings without ever leaving home. If you have skills and expertise that can be valuable to others, with a few keystrokes on your computer, you can tell the whole world about them. Once you start doing business on the Internet, in just a few hours or a few days you can start receiving requests for your products or services from all over the world.

The Internet's growth rate is so rapid that most information published in paper form about the Internet is outdated by the time it reaches the press. Don't be discouraged. With an Internet connection, you can get the most current demographic figures. See the appendices for Internet addresses that will help you find the latest information.

# Chapter 4

## Disappearing Domain Names

Leaving statistics behind, the Internet growth can be demonstrated under purely practical circumstances — the growth in the number of domain names issued. A domain name is the name by which a person or company is known in cyberspace on the Internet. Most individuals and even most businesses do not have their own domain name, but a large business that is going to be a serious player in cyberspace needs its own domain name. A company with its own domain name commands respect and shows a definite presence on the Net. The domain name becomes part of the Internet address for all correspondence flowing to or from anyone at the company, just as a city name is part of the postal address.

If you had applied for a domain name during January 1995, you would have been told that there was at least a four-week wait. The wait was long because more than two thousand domain name applications were being filed every day, and InterNIC, the organization that assigns and keeps track of domain names, wasn't expecting such a large number of applications. InterNIC has since automated the process of registering domain names, so the turnaround time is much quicker. You can apply for domain names through your local provider (the company you use to connect to the Internet). There is a yearly charge, which is due up-front, to maintain registration of a domain name with InterNIC.

A domain name, which consists of a series of letters and/or numbers, forms part of your Internet address. The actual domain part of the address is the part that falls after the @ symbol. People can find you on the Net by entering your "address" in a dialog box. For example, the authors of *Superhighway to Wealth* can be reached at *ww@infodirect.com*. In this address, "ww" is the user name, and "infodirect" is the domain name. InfoDirect, Inc., is the name of the company that developed *Superhighway to Wealth*. Sometimes there will be numbers and letters combined with dots, slashes, or underscores that will establish a pathway leading to information located on the computer where the domain name address is maintained. It is important to note that the address should be copied exactly.

In InfoDirect's address, the ".com" is the "top level domain." The top level domain suggests what type of organization you are dealing with on the Internet. Common top-level domain codes include the following:

| CODE | DESCRIPTION |
| --- | --- |
| edu | educational institutions |
| gov | government |
| mil | military |
| org | miscellaneous organizations |
| net | network organizations |
| com | commercial |

The top level domain code is part of every Internet address. It is not *always* a correct description or indication of the organization, however. For instance, some commercial businesses have ".org" or ".edu" as part of their addresses. This is because top level domain codes are used only to identify the computer and the chain of responsibility for that computer system's connection to the Internet. All businesses, schools, etc., using the same computer to store their Internet information will have the same top level domain. In the United States, the top level domain ends with the organization code. In all other countries, the top level domain includes a two letter country code after the organization code. For example, ".ca" identifies Canada, and ".jp" identifies Japan.

Each domain name used on the worldwide Internet system has to be absolutely unique. Once a domain name is claimed, it is gone. Remember that domain names are claimed worldwide. The domain name InfoDirect, for example, has been registered with InterNIC, and no one else anywhere in the world can claim that name.

In the early days of the Internet, anyone could register any domain name. All of the names were simply "up for grabs." Some people tried to capitalize on the unrestricted registration process by claiming trademarked names as their own. The name grabbing rush became known as the "Internet Domain Name Gold Rush." It is now shaping up to be a trademark headache with courts attempting to control the theft of trademarked names and dispense justice in a formerly unrestricted process. There have been requests for InterNIC to become a Internet policing agency by doing an expensive trademark search for every domain name application they issue. According to Lynne Beresford, the Patent and Trademark Office (PTO) legal administrator, the PTO is recommending a policy of denying a grant of a domain name to a company that has not previously trademarked that name. This policy has not yet been accepted, but most trademark attorneys predict that it will soon be adopted as law. Even so, InterNIC issues a warning on its registration page about trying to claim a name in cyberspace that is trademarked in the real world.

Progressive companies have begun placing their domain addresses on all of their letterheads and advertising, including TV commercials, making their products more accessible to the wise consumer. Domain addresses provide another excellent way for an organization to build name recognition and a ready connection with the public. A name has a powerful influence when marketing a product. Like a clever or descriptive 800 number, a domain name will be easier to remember if it is closely associated with the company's name or one of its well-known products. A recognizable domain name will enable a company to take advantage of the Internet market, present a professional image, and make money.

# Section II

# Tools

# Tools

Graphical browsers such as Mosaic and Netscape made the Internet easy to use because everything is done with point and click graphics. To get all the advantages the Internet offers, it is important to understand each of the different Internet tools and how to use them. In spite of popular belief, doing business over the Internet requires a knowledge of each of the basic Internet tools, not just the World Wide Web. Once each of the Internet tools is understood, it is easy to envision how the different tools can be utilized to create a powerful and strategic marketing plan for any Internet business venture. The more unique the marketing effort is, the more successful the business can be. Willingness to think in new ways coupled with imagination is the key to success in making money on the Internet. Before any plan can even be imagined, a good knowledge of the tools that will be used to build the plan is a necessity.

The basic Internet tools are: E-mail, the World Wide Web, Gopher, FTP, Usenet (Newsgroups), Online Commercial Services, and Bulletin Board Systems (BBSs) .

# Chapter 5

## E-mail

E-mail is electronic mail or mail which is sent by computer over a network.  Lots of companies have networks, and they use e-mail to send messages back and forth within the company.  The grand-daddy of all networks is the Internet. The Internet allows e-mail to be sent to millions of people around the world, not just within a company's network.  E-mail is currently the most widely used Internet tool.  The Internet was originally developed to insure uninterrupted communication for the government, and e-mail was one of the first and most important applications developed. Today communication by e-mail is one of the core strengths of the Internet.

Businesses use e-mail in a wide variety of ways.  E-mail is used internally within a company to keep departments, work groups, and individuals in close contact. It is also used to keep in touch, nationally and internationally, with sales representatives, suppliers, information brokers, and customers. E-mail saves both time and money compared to traditional means of communication. An e-mail message can be one page long or 100 pages long. It doesn't matter. The only cost of e-mail is the local Internet connection cost. For a few pennies, literally tens of thousands of letters can be sent simultaneously using e-mail, and each letter will arrive almost instantly because it is traveling through the Internet at the speed of light. It is an understatement to say that e-mail travels significantly faster than the regular postal mail or "snail mail," as netters call the postal mail. E-mail is truly breaking down the barriers of time and distance that hampered business communication in the past.

## E-mail Addresses

In order to receive e-mail, you need an e-mail address. E-mail addresses are usually numbers, letters, or a combination of both. In the middle of the numbers and letters there is always an "@" symbol. Everything to the left of the @ symbol is considered the "user name."

Everything to the right of the @ symbol is considered the domain part of the address. The "domain name" is the part of the domain which tells the world what computer the e-mail address is located on. E-mail addresses can be short or long.

If you want to write Lee and Kristy Phillips about one of their other books, *Trust Me! The Truth About Living Revocable Trusts*, you can send an e-mail message to: *lee@legalees.com*. This is a short address. The important thing to remember is to type the address exactly as it appears. Of course, it is impressive to have an e-mail address that has your own domain name. An e-mail address like *Kristy@Phillips.com* suggests that "Wow, she is really into the Internet."

## Signature Files

Signature files are usually short files that can be added to your e-mail letters to act as a letter head or logo. They usually appear at the end of the message. Most computer programs that send e-mail can be programmed to automatically add a signature file to every e-mail message sent.

Signature files are an acceptable way to advertise or make a statement with each letter that goes out over the Internet. The signature file will often give the person's telephone number and street address along with a slogan, or statement. This lets people get in touch using conventional means of communication. Go ahead and use the signature file to refer people to your other Internet addresses and even a toll-free phone number or a fax line number. Some people are still more comfortable using a fax than they are using e-mail, and a fax number enables them to contact you. By the way, it has been said that very soon the fax machine will take its place in history with the ditto machine and the adding machine, as people become more comfortable with e-mail. Two examples of signature files follow.

InfoDirect is the company where Lee and Kristy work. In addition to publishing *Superhighway to Wealth*, InfoDirect has developed a very comprehensive Internet training package called *WorldWalk*™. InfoDirect's signature file is straightforward and businesslike. It's used on e-mail messages sent from the staff at InfoDirect when they answer e-mail sent to the company. The following is the InfoDirect signature file:

/\/\/\/\/\/\/\/\/\/\/\/\/\/\/\/\/\/\/\/\/\/\/\/\/\/\/\/\/\/\/\/\/\/\/\/\

InfoDirect, Inc.
ww@infodirect.com
470 No. University Ave Ste 203
Provo, UT 84601
http://worldwalk.com

The signature file below is added to Lee's posted messages on the Techno-L listserv (a part of the Internet where people interested in technology transfer exchange views). As an expert in technology transfer, Lee has developed licensing software that is easy-to-use and allows "non-experts" to write very professional patent license agreements. Although the Techno-L group is interested in tech transfer and many of them are involved in licensing, they do not want to receive unsolicited e-mail about his software. When Lee responds to issues under discussion, however, his signature file indicates that he is the creator of the License Preparation System™. As he interacts with the group and posts cogent, helpful answers, his signature file becomes familiar to people in the group. Those members of the list who are curious about the License Preparation System can e-mail him directly or visit his other Internet address to find out more about the software. Lee is advertising, but it is not offensive to the members of the group.

> Lee R. Phillips
> The License Preparation System
> Software to write licenses: fast and professionally
> "If you are going to license technology, you ought to use the technology of licensing -The License Preparation System"
> (801) 377-5952
> http://legalees.com

---

***Marketing Tip:*** *Do add a signature file to your e-mail address. Include enough information that you will have name recognition on the Internet. It shouldn't be longer than six or seven lines nor be so "cute" that it becomes annoying. Some people like to include meaningful quotations as part of their signatures. If you decide to do that, choose carefully.*

---

## Mail Lists

Loyal customers are one of a business' most valuable assets. Every business needs to "cultivate" its customers and should be carefully keeping track of each customer's name and address. In addition to the customer's street address, e-mail addresses now need to be collected for each customer. Every form that captures a customer's snail mail address (their real world address), needs to be reworked so that it will also capture their e-mail address.

Any list of people you want to mail to can easily be put in a mail list file for e-mailing. E-mail programs allow you to type your letter and hit one button to send the same letter to the entire list. It doesn't matter if there are two or 2,000 people on the list, each person gets the letter instantly. Of course, it doesn't cost anymore to e-mail to 2,000 than it does to just two.

Using e-mail techniques, news can travel from person to person across the Internet in an unbelievable cascade. A piece of news can be entered on a single computer, and with the stroke of a computer key, it can be sent to everyone on a mail list. As each person gets the letter in their e-mail box, they can forward the letter to everyone on their mail lists by simply using the "forward" feature of their e-mail program. They don't have to retype the letter or even read it.

When a flaw was discovered in the Pentium chip Intel makes for computers, the whole world knew about it instantly. Intel's nightmare came long before the first newspaper printed the news. Netters started to "put out the word" and within only a few hours, millions of people had received e-mail exposing the flaw. The news cascaded through the Internet at an unbelievable rate.

## Mailbot (Autoresponder)

A logical enhancement in the use of e-mail is the mailbot. A mailbot is a computer program that automatically answers e-mail sent to a specific address. It is neat because a mailbot can be set up to shoot answers back to potential customers automatically. A mailbot can deliver the most recent information in a matter of minutes, 24 hours a day, all year round. A customer can request specific information from an e-mail address, and the mailbot will make the information instantly available.

In an age when fast responses can really make the difference in a sale, a mailbot makes a lot of sense. When a potential customer contacts a mailbot via e-mail, the 'bot acts like a "robot" and sends a prepared document, news, or sales letter back to the person making the contact. This creates a built-in self-selected target market of those people who contacted the 'bot.

The 'bot can also gather valuable client information, such as the names and e-mail addresses of those who contact it. This service provides the beginning of a database or mail list of potential clients. A mail list can literally be collected 24 hours a day. Each name can be stored and followed up with further communication. A 'bot can also log the activity of an account. It can keep track of times and the nature of contacts. Of course, it also can keep track of how many contacts are made, and how the person making the contact discovered the business's advertising. This type of data may help in test marketing. Businesses can tell right away what sort of copy, information, or newsletter pulls in the responses. The 'bot can even collect street addresses so the business will know where its customers live. Best of all, changes can be made quickly to any aspect of an automated response/advertisement in order to improve performance.

It is also possible to restrict access to a 'bot by creating a password system that only lets authorized users access the 'bot. With restricted access, the 'bot can be used to make confidential information available to distributors, sales people, manufacturers, and other people that need information. Those people can come and get the information any time they wish from anywhere in the world.

Mailbots can be very powerful business tools. Think of the potential the enhanced instant communication capabilities of a mailbot could give you. Of course, mailbots can be used with the other Internet tools to create an unbeatable business strategy.

## Listservs

Another easy way to enhance personal and business-related communication is to use a listserv. Listservs are an extension of e-mail and mailbots. The listservs can be thought of as the newsletters of the Internet. "Servers" are computers that "serve" information over the Internet. "Listservs" are computers that automatically serve information to the list of names maintained by the computer. Each e-mail address on the list will automatically receive each piece of information sent out by the listserv.

Companies are setting up listservs for their internal networks. The listserv makes it easy to communicate with groups in the company. For example, anyone in the company design group can "post" or submit a notice or letter to the listserv and the posting will automatically be sent to everyone on the company's design list.

The same concept works over the Internet. If you want to be updated on the latest ideas about the use of your computer printer, you can subscribe to the listserv that puts out information related to the printer. Anyone who has a good idea (or a not-so-good idea) can post their idea to the listserv, and the idea will automatically be sent to everyone who has their name on the list.

Note that you "subscribe" to have your name put on the list. Listservs aren't like junk mail because you subscribe to the list. Names are not just randomly or secretly put on the list. You have to take a specific action to get your name on a list, and you can take your name off the list anytime you want. The "articles" that come across the listserv are like ongoing editorials or letters to the editor.

Many listservs keep the postings for a long time in archive files. The archives can be very useful because a huge base of information is available. Professionals, scientists, and businesses can subscribe to listservs with very narrow topics, and the information available in the archives can be invaluable. By sifting through the archives, dozens of people's opinions can be obtained on the exact topic that interests you, provided the topic has been previously tossed around by members of the listserv.

Using a listserv, you can literally ask the world a question. It works this way: a person poses a problem or topic for discussion to the list, then other list members post their replies, offer help or advice, or share their expertise. Of course, each posting is e-mailed to everyone on the list, so that each member can follow the exchange of information. Some topics may be vitally interesting to a specific member. Others are of no interest and can be quickly deleted.

Subscribing to a listserv is easy. Listservs are setup so that anyone can subscribe by simply sending an e-mail message to the listserv address.

Administrative addresses used for subscribing to listservs tend to appear in one of the following three formats:

←*listserv@domain.name*

←*majordomo@domain.name*

←*listproc@domain.name*

Commands such as *info, help, get, subscribe, list,* etc. should be sent to the administrative addresses in order to get a response. Usually, postings or responses that are to be sent to the list of subscribers will be sent to a different address.

When you first subscribe to a listserv, the listserv may ask for your snail mail address and other information before it will actually put your e-mail address on the list. Obviously, the marketers using the listserv are doing their marketing research. They're making good use of the listserv as a marketing tool by collecting information about you.

Whenever you sign onto a listserv, make sure you get a copy of the Frequently Asked Questions, or FAQs (pronounced "fax"), so that you can at least get the procedure necessary to unsubscribe if you want to get your name off the list. Also, the FAQs will help you understand the list's rules so you don't embarrass yourself when you post a reply on the listserv.

One of the disadvantages of subscribing to a listserv is the potential volume of e-mail you will get if the list is an active group—you can be inundated with list mail which will fill up lots of disk space. However, good listservs are worth the few minutes it takes to electronically sort through your mail. The *Superhighway to Wealth* appendices list some listservs which are devoted to business and business-related topics.

---

***Marketing Tip:*** *Send for a list of Internet mailing lists by sending an e-mail message to LISTSERV@LISTSERV.NET. Leave the subject blank. In the body of the message type LIST GLOBAL. You'll receive a reply within a day or two. The list is LARGE. Look it over and subscribe to lists that interest you and which might be useful to your marketing strategy.*
*You can also search for lists by using the search engines at* http://www.sblegal.com/sunburst/maillist.html
*You can subscribe to the lists directly from these Web sites.*

---

# Chapter 6

## World Wide Web

The World Wide Web (WWW or just the Web) is the hottest development in cyberspace. The Web's growth has been astounding with thousands of new users setting up stores, information centers, advertisements and other types of Web sites every day. What attracts all these new users? According to the Nielsen Media Research survey, approximately half of all netters use the Web for business purposes, such as gathering information, researching competitors, collaborating with others, communicating internationally, and providing customer/vendor support. Apparently the Web is also catching the eye of consumers, because millions of purchases are being made over the Internet, and the bulk of them are being made on the Web.

The Web is by far the most exciting and interesting Internet feature, and it has the potential to become the best marketing tool available to businesses. Consumer groups are openly stating, and even testifying before Congress, that the Web is a far more powerful advertising medium than television. Actually, the Web is powerful for a lot of purposes in addition to marketing and advertising.

The Web links together thousands of servers (computers), and each server contains a small portion of the Web's total information base. These servers are connected through an agreed-upon protocol, HyperText Transfer Protocol (HTTP), which is the primary language of the Web. The software program or interface which is used to explore the World Wide Web is called a browser. The most popular browsers are Netscape Navigator, Mosaic, and Microsoft Explorer. Your access provider will probably supply you with a browser when you sign up. Browsers are also available free on the Internet, and can be "downloaded" or brought into your computer as soon as you are properly connected to the Internet.

In technical terms, the World Wide Web is officially described as a "wide-area hyper media information retrieval initiative aiming to give universal access to a large universe of documents." Put simply, the Web is a community of linked online information resources that appear in many different media forms. The media forms not only include text, which is used by the other programs on the Internet, they also include color pictures, sound, videos, and, since Synthonics' creation, even stereo 3D interactive images. The online resources not only include information maintained by businesses, but also libraries, museums, service organizations, magazines, governments, and even individuals.

Resources for businesses and consumers—people doing business on the Net—are the fastest growing segment of the Web. Commercial growth has been phenomenal. There were 588 commercial sites in September of 1994. By April 1995, there were over 6000. At the end of November 1995, there were 17,489 commercial sites; 1223 of which were listed in one week! Today, businesses are scrambling to figure out how to use the Internet and take advantage of the Web. They may not have thought of the formula P=KC (Power = Knowledge x speed of light), but they can sense that the Web holds a huge power potential.

## URLs

Each location or Web site has a unique address on the Internet. Web browsers all have some type of prompt which asks for the Web site address you want the browser to locate. When the address is entered in response to the prompt, the browser locates the site and brings its contents back to your computer. Web addresses are called URLs (Universal Resource Locators). URLs indicate what the server is, where it is located, and where on that server the requested information is to be found. An example of a URL is *http://worldwalk.com*

The first letters in the URL indicate the type of server which will be accessed. "Http" at the beginning of the address signifies a Web server. Other Internet server formats such as Gopher, FTP, and Telnet sites can also be accessed using Netscape or Mosaic by identifying the desired server before the colon in the URL. After the two forward slashes, the location of the site is designated. In the example above, *WorldWalk*™ is the site and *worldwalk.com* is the domain name. (*WorldWalk*™ is an Internet training course with simple workbooks and video instruction that InfoDirect has created.) There may be additional forward slashes and site designations in an address. Each designation gives more detailed information about the exact location of the requested site. Some additional examples of URLs include:

A simple Website address:

*http://www.legalees.com*

Project 2000's URL for marketing sites:

*http://www2000.ogsm.vanderbilt.edu/*
*eli.cga?ffcfffff.ffffffff+ 7#21*

Business Resources:

*gopher://gopher.nijenrode.nl*

Internet Society

*ftp://ftp.isoc.org*

Economic BBS

*telnet://ebb.stat-usa.gov*

## Hypertext Links

When you visit a Web site, you'll see underlined or highlighted words or graphics that are made to stand out from the rest of the text. As was discussed earlier, these are called hypertext links or "hyperlinks." Hyperlinks have Internet addresses hidden behind them. If you could "lift up" the hyperlinks, you would see a URL code hidden behind the highlighted text. You don't see the URL, but your computer does, and when you click your mouse on a hyperlink, it takes you to the site of the hidden URL, and the information located there is automatically displayed. The Web site which contains the hyperlinked words or graphic is said to be "linked" to the location designated by the hidden URL. Hypertext can link to all kinds of locations and documents.

In order to explain how hyperlinks work, imagine cruising the Internet and finding a Web site devoted to NBA basketball. There the names of several NBA teams are highlighted in a different color. The Utah Jazz is one of the highlighted names. The text of the NBA Web site reads, "The **Utah Jazz** are closing in on the NBA record for most consecutive road games won." Click on the words, "Utah Jazz," which are a hyperlink, and immediately the computer displays a "page" or "site" devoted to the Utah Jazz. This page contains information about the Jazz, their consecutive road game winning streak, John Stockton's record-breaking number of assists, and a score box from their last game. The Utah Jazz page also gives information about upcoming games with other teams, such as the San Antonio Spurs.

The Spurs' name is highlighted, signifying that it is a hyperlink which leads to news and information about the Spurs.

At the Jazz site, there might be a picture of Karl Malone dunking the basketball over Dennis Rodman. A sound clip could be linked to this picture. Clicking on the picture, which is itself a hyperlink, will result in a roar from your computer's speakers, and you can hear the crowd's reaction to Malone's dunk.

On the Spurs' page is a picture of David Robinson (the "Admiral") of the Spurs. Click on the picture and a biography, complete with pictures depicting aspects of the Admiral's career will appear on the screen. At the bottom of the page the word Navy is highlighted in a paragraph about Robinson's college days at the Naval Academy. A click on the word Navy leads to the Naval Academy's Web site, which even contains recruiting information and a sign-up form.

You can probably sense that following hyperlinks can literally lead you on an endless adventure through cyberspace.

## Web Sites

World Wide Web sites are also commonly referred to as "Web sites," "home pages," and "storefronts." Businesses use Web sites as electronic stores or catalogs in cyberspace. On its Web site, a business can place its logo, colorful graphics, information regarding its services and products, sound clips, video clips, and of course, order forms. If it is placed in a high traffic area of the Web and properly promoted, the Web site may be seen by tens of millions of potential customers. Think of a Web site as a global electronic display ad that is working 24 hours a day, seven days a week, 365 days a year, dispensing sales information and collecting orders. All of this is done by computer. Many businesses have someone available during office hours to handle orders and answer questions generated by the Web site, but almost all business tasks related to a Web site can be handled automatically over the Internet, without any personnel. Using the Internet's technology can save a business time and money in addition to making money on the Superhighway.

InfoDirect uses the Internet to communicate with customers all over the world and to communicate with its business contacts in the Philippines and Guam. It sends contracts by FTP, and as e-mail attachments, anywhere in the world in just a few minutes. Much of InfoDirect's customer support is conducted over the Internet, and it's virtually free. Customers can receive answers to their questions in a matter of minutes or hours, and they don't have to pay for long distance calls or wait on hold. When companies use the Internet, both the company and customer save money on long distance charges, postage, and paper. Plus, they save time because communication is instantaneous. No more telephone tag or having to wait until the middle of the night to call overseas. Turnaround time for fulfillment of orders is shortened from weeks to days. The Internet is changing the concept of mail and overnight packages. Some states' laws already recognize a document received via e-mail as a valid legal document under many circumstances.

***Marketing Tip:*** *If you are thinking about setting up a Web site, visit lots of other Web sites. You'll get ideas for what works and what doesn't. Try to avoid complex graphics, because they take a long time to transmit over the Internet, and viewers often become frustrated and won't wait to see the full Web site. Web sites should be interesting and informative. Give customers a reason to come back by offering sales or information that periodically changes.*

## Cybermalls

As with any advertisement or store, the goal in cyberspace is to get customers to see the ad or visit the store and buy. Often business owners find that they get more traffic to their site if they place their Web site in a good cybermall—one that has lots of visitors and excellent customer support. A cybermall is much like the mall in your home town. However, instead of a collection of physical stores, it is a collection of electronic storefronts. Good cybermalls have a large variety of products and services on a series of Web site ads that can be accessed by millions of consumers all over the world. Good cybermalls offer state-of-the-art electronic shopping. Imagine the fun of being able to browse and shop at boutiques throughout the world without leaving home.

What makes a great cybermall? First, look at the size and profile of the mall. Is the mall a high profile place that shoppers have heard about? One of the ways to determine its size and popularity is to ask how many "hits" or visitors it has each day. You can also take a look at prizes, awards, and ratings it has received from groups such as Lycos, Point, Magellan, *i*nfoseek, etc.

A quality mall carries a diverse number of products and has a directory searching system which allows shoppers to easily find what they are looking for. A good cybermall also has the technology necessary to carry on a large Internet business. It should have plenty of storage space and access lines. The successful malls have encrypted, secure, easy-to-use order forms as well as interactive features. Customers like to interact with the mall and its stores. The mall should also offer areas where the consumer continues to return for updated information.

Any business can have a Web site made and advertise over the Internet. The major online services (CompuServe, AOL, Prodigy) provide areas where Web sites can be "posted." Additionally, your local Internet Service Provider (ISP) will often provide space for Web sites on their system. However, putting a Web site in a cybermall gives you a bigger advantage because much of the advertising that you would have to do to get people to visit your site is already being done by the mall itself. The mall should have high visibility and an established clientele. And, any extra advertising that you do yourself will only increase sales.

There are many cybermalls out there. Some are better than others. As an example of a cybermall, look at Access Market Square *(http://amsquare.com)* which is one of the top cybermalls. It is also one of the oldest malls on the Internet. Access Market Square has a colorful graphic representation of a mall and dozens of store categories listed on its welcoming page. Clicking on one of the store categories quickly displays a list of stores that have products in that category. Each store is represented by its own colorful icon or logo. Clicking on one of the logos instantly displays the store with pictures and descriptions of its products. Access Market Square has stores offering everything from hand-painted Hawaiian scarves to toner cartridges for laser printers. Access Market Square also has a classified ad section where everything, including an old saxophone is advertised and sold. Classified ads in the mall can be up to one hundred words long. Access Market Square is a very popular spot on the Internet because almost anything and everything imaginable is for sale there.

Even with thousands of products for sale in the mall, it is easy to find any specific item. Access Market Square has an elaborate search engine that searches through the entire mall. Searches can be performed by type of item, brand name, product type, or store name. Access Market Square has a feature known as "shopping cart technology" which allows a shopper to check out from multiple stores with one transaction. The mall has a monthly contest and a "What's New" feature which keeps customers coming back. It also has the latest encryption systems so customers will not be reluctant to give their credit card numbers over the Internet.

On the colorful Access Market Square welcome page there is a row of icons that display some of the awards that have been given to Access Market Square by prestigious reviewing groups. Point's Review lists Access Market Square in the top 5% of all Web sites. Riddler's Choice, *i*nfoseek, Magellan, and the All-Internet Shopping Directory have all given Access Market Square their highest awards.

Access Market Square is only one of hundreds of malls in cyberspace, but it is one of the most advanced, popular malls and can be used as a standard to evaluate other malls. Anyone wanting to place a Web site in a cybermall should check out the mall's features before placing an advertisement there.

# Chapter 7

## Gopher

Thousands of computers on the Internet hold massive amounts of information that is yours for the taking—if you know how to find what you want. Much of the information available is organized so it can be searched quickly by reviewing the table of contents or "menu" of the information stored on each computer.

Gopher is the aptly-named menu searcher of cyberspace. Gopher can only search information which has been organized in the computer's storage space using the Gopher menu format. It is an older Internet technology, which means most of the information organized in Gopher format or "Gopherspace" is going to be text, not pictures.

Gopher was developed at the University of Minnesota. The mascot of Minnesota just happens to be a gopher—hence the name for this handy searching tool that digs through volumes of information to find exactly what you want. Gopher starts searching in general menus and narrows its search to increasingly more specific menus. There aren't any fancy graphics to click on, so Gopher is perceived as being harder to use than the World Wide Web. Because Gopher brings up a menu and allows you to progress one menu at a time, you can get where you want to go rather easily. Gopher is a very valuable Internet tool to master, and it is easy to use after just a little practice.

A good way of picturing how Gopher works is to think of a simple search for a book at your local library. The first "menu" is very general, i.e., author, subject, or title. After you make your selection, another menu appears. You then make additional selections until the description, location, and status of the book you want is narrowed down sufficiently so that all you need to do is walk to the shelf and pick it up.

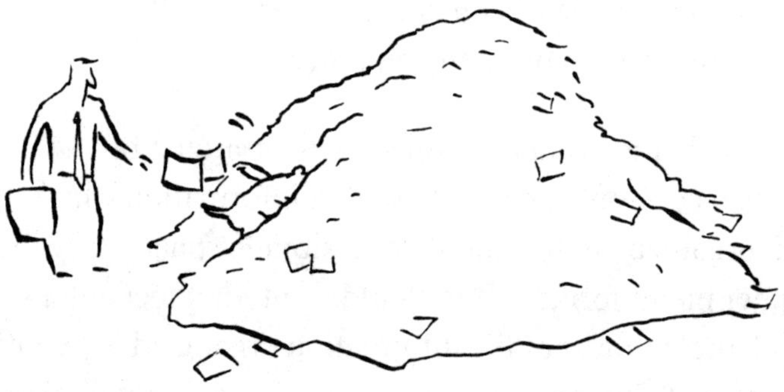

gopher

Gopher is valuable for many business tasks. It can be used to do copyright and trademark searches. It can help find local job listings. It can provide you with travel information on possible problems in politically unstable areas you might have on your itinerary. Journalists use it to get story leads. One journalist uses Gopher to find an interesting article stored in cyberspace, and then he contacts the article's author directly for interviews or further information on late-breaking developments. The National Science Foundation keeps an archive of abstracts on research projects which may speed your business research. The ways Gopher can help a business are limited only by the imagination of the business. Keyword searches using Gopher can lead to interesting articles on every topic you can imagine.

A big mistake businesses make is totally dismissing Gopher and assuming the only place to do business is on the World Wide Web. Most businesses would benefit from having both a World Wide Web site and a Gopher site. The Gopher site can offer the same information as the Web site, but its content is usually in text format. The information has to be placed in the computer so Gopher can find it. Although it is possible to transmit graphics, sound and video clips to your Gopher customers, this cannot be done "interactively," as can be done on the Web. Graphics, sound, and video found by Gopher must be downloaded and then accessed offline. Even though Gopher is not as attractive as a World Wide Web site, businesses need to remember that many people who are online at any given time don't have the capability of accessing Web sites. You wouldn't want to miss a very large target market by ignoring the possibility of a Gopher site, even if the only thing these potential customers can see online is text.

An interesting example of a Gopher site is at the rock band *Live (gopher:// mediafive.yyz.com)* site. The band's site leads to a discography, transcriptions of interviews, back issues of e-mailing list digests, tour information, and song lyrics.

Many Internet travelers use the Net to gather information in order to make a decision about a purchase they make in the traditional ways. For this reason alone, a Gopher site can be very valuable to a business. Electronic files can be accessed by interested buyers who are very specific about the kind of information they desire. These files can contain such diverse information as product description, clipped articles about the business and/or the product, lists of locations where the product is found, seminar dates and registration information, customer feedback, success stories, biographies of the developers, and excerpts of articles or books that will entice the reader to want to know more. Use of Gopher in this manner is a good way to boost sales and credibility. Whether the sale is made over the Internet or in the local store, it's still a sale, and Gopher should be another valuable tool in every business' package of marketing strategies.

# Chapter 8

## File Transfer Protocol (FTP)

With all the excitement created by graphical browsers such as Netscape, Mosaic, and Microsoft Explorer why would anyone want to use FTP? FTP stands for File Transfer Protocol. It is the backbone of the Net and traditionally has been the Net's most widely used feature. Using FTP, your computer reaches through the Internet into another computer's files and literally takes what you need, brings it back to your computer, and stores it in your computer's files. The computer that stores the files for you to reach out and take is called the "remote host," and the computer that is doing the taking is called the "local host." Each day thousands of hosts transfer files all over the world. Most of the information available for FTP transfer is free, and of course, the transfer takes place in only seconds.

With all this free information, will the selling of information become obsolete? Absolutely not! There is a lot of free information available on the Internet. However,

FTP also makes mountains of valuable information available for a fee. This is a resource which should not be overlooked. For example, anyone who organizes a well-written and well-developed electronic newsletter or article will be appreciated by those customers who don't have the time to do that kind of research or who could more effectively use their time on other projects. They are happy to pay for the information in the newsletter or article. FTP makes the information available to them 24 hours a day. Some businesses are making a lot of money selling information they make available through FTP files.

ftp

Businesses can benefit from using FTP in a number of other ways. For example, there are millions of people cruising the Internet every day looking for FTP information. That's a huge potential target to which the business can advertise or more subtly promote itself, its products, or services. Businesses should certainly consider having an FTP site for advertising and to supply customers, vendors, and their own personnel with information.

FTP is probably the quickest way to retrieve files on the Internet, but there is a catch to using FTP. The World Wide Web lets netters see the pretty pictures, and even Gopher lets netters read and review text they find. FTP on the other hand, won't let the user view any files or information over the Internet. The file must be brought over the Internet and stored in the netter's computer before the file can be viewed. FTP only displays the names of the files available on the specific remote host computer accessed through FTP.

In order to retrieve a file using FTP you have to know all of the location information concerning the file. You have to know which computer the file is located on, the directory it is found in, and the exact name of the file. This information can be obtained through a Gopher search, or you have to be given the information by some source such as a Web site, friend, magazine, book, etc.

Businesses should keep a list of FTP sites where they can get information that is timely and valuable to them. For example, many software packages are routinely updated for their users from FTP sites. FTP sites that have service information, new product releases, and other pieces of important information should be visited often.

An FTP site can help businesses do "secondary marketing" as well as provide the capability of giving excellent customer support. The business can keep files at its FTP site concerning product improvements, price lists, sales literature, order forms, gifts, contests, and catalogs. Even a few chapters of a book, sound and video clips, and Frequently Asked Questions (FAQs) about products can be put on FTP sites where customers and potential customers can come and get them at any time. FTP files are frequently used to offer clients technical support because the files are available whenever they are needed. The business doesn't have to provide any personnel to "give" the technical support and clients can retrieve the support files whenever it's convenient.

Another business advantage of an FTP site is the possibility it offers to capture the e-mail addresses of all those who visit the site. Typically netters go to an FTP site and gain access to the site as an "anonymous" user. Then the netter is asked for a password, which is usually his e-mail address. This means that all the netters (customers) who come to the site are required to leave their e-mail address. The company sponsoring the FTP site thus is building an electronic mailing list of people who have already expressed an interest in its products by visiting the site. The company can follow up with sales letters that can be sent and received in just minutes. So not only does the company have a preselected mailing list, it also has the advantage of being able to communicate with its potential clients immediately while they are most interested. Instead of days and weeks passing by as it would with snail mail, the business can follow up and close the sale right away.

FTP doesn't offer any mechanism to allow users to move from computer to computer like Gopher does. In a Gopher search the menus explored are usually stored in different computers in different locations somewhere in the world. The Gopher jumps from computer to computer. FTP only makes the first big jump to the site. Once in the host computer's files, you can do some poking around in the files that are located there. Does that mean that you can go to any company's files and look at whatever you want? Or, that anyone with a computer and an Internet connection can go through all of your business documents? No! Companies typically keep the files they are willing to let you look at in a subdirectory called *"/pub"* for public. That means that anonymous logins (users) are free to look at and access these public files, but they will be denied access to all other company files. Companies are spending big bucks to build "firewalls" in their computers to insure that users coming to their computer can't get to the parts of the computer protected from the public. Some FTP sites are not open to the public (anonymous logins), and all users must be authorized and register with the company in order to gain access to their files.

What if you are using a computer system, such as at work, or at a university, which only gives you access to e-mail? Can you still take advantage of FTP? Most emphatically, yes! You can e-mail your requests for FTP files to any computer that acts as an FTP mail server (such as FTP mail@decwrl.dec.com). Of course you'll have to know where the file is and what its name is, but the FTP mail server computer will retrieve the requested file and mail it back to you by e-mail in a few minutes or a few days.

With FTP you can download unlimited amounts of information, and software such as Web browsers, newsreaders, utilities, etc.

***Marketing Tip:*** *Set up an FTP site which is linked to your Web site, and have free information available for visitors to your site. You'll gain credibility and interest in your product. If you have an electronic catalog, put it in the FTP site. Catalog sales on the Internet are in their infancy, so now is a great time to become involved. According to the Direct Marketing Association, in 1995 total non-Internet catalog purchases exceeded $62 billion - up $14 billion from the year before. (Direct Marketing Association) As more and more netters shop online, catalog sales on the Internet are bound to jump.*

# Chapter 9

## Usenet (Newsgroups)

The Usenet newsgroups are similar to the bulletin boards at the local supermarket or in a school. Anyone can post a message for all to see. Internet newsgroups use the Internet to make their bulletin board format available to interested readers throughout the world. Like the Listservs, the newsgroups have one-to-many communication, but the Usenet communications are not e-mail based. Instead, the newsgroups are accessed through a newsreader program. Newsreader software is available through your access provider or free over the Internet.

To envision how a newsgroup works, imagine a large bulletin board where someone has posted a topic for discussion such as motorcycles. Anyone in the world who wants to talk about motorcycles can participate in this discussion. In order to participate or "subscribe" to the newsgroup, simply click on the newsgroup title from the list of available newsgroups (there are more than 14,000 of them). The list is located on your provider's computer and is accessed using the newsreader program. Subscribing to a newsgroup means that you have added the group to the list of groups you have selected for your newsreader interface to manage. You don't really go through any formal subscription process or pay any fees; you just click on the newsgroup title and that lets you into the group as a participating member. Anyone who has subscribed to the group can read all of the messages and put up, or "post," messages on the electronic bulletin board. The messages are posted on the local server which then routes them all over the world to other servers. Then anyone who wants to read the messages can subscribe to the group and read them. When you don't want to read the group's messages anymore, you simply unsubscribe.

There are discussion groups for just about any topic imaginable. They are usually divided into hierarchies such as:

| | |
|---|---|
| comp | computer-related topics |
| news | topics relating to the newsgroups, announcements of newsgroups |
| rec | games, arts, pets, Star Trek, music, sports, hobbies |
| sci | science-related topics |
| soc | social interactions, various cultures, history, politics, religion, feminism, roots |
| talk | hot topics for discussion, archived discussions, largely debate-oriented |
| alt | subjects of a personal nature or current issues. |
| bionet | topics for biologists |
| biz | business-related topics |
| bit | redistribution of Bitnet |

In addition, there are other specialized lists, some of which may require a subscription fee, but the categories listed above are the most commonly used.

Returning to the motorcycle topic, if you want to discuss dirt bikes, you would subscribe to the newsgroup named *rec.motorcycles.dirt*. While looking at the list, you notice that there are several other groups that discuss motorcycles: *rec.motorcycles.harley* and *rec.motorcycles.racing*. You could also subscribe to these related newsgroups. After a quick look at the *.harley* group, it does not appear to qualify. You could unsubscribe to that one, but remain subscribed to the others.

With literally millions of users accessing the Usenet newsgroups every day, the advantages to the business community seem obvious. Why not simply compose an ad for your product and post it to every newsgroup on the Internet? This may sound tempting, but don't do it! "Spamming," as this practice is called, is almost universally despised. The three or four people who encourage it and have tried it out in the past are being harassed off the Net. If you plan to advertise in the newsgroups, look for the appropriate places, like the *misc.forsale* and the *biz* groups.

***Marketing Tip:*** *Look through Usenet newsgroups for topics related to your product or service. Read the messages for a few days to see if the group is interested in your kind of offering before you post. It's a good idea to participate in the discussions for a while first before you talk about your product. Then you'll have some sort of "identity" if and when you find it appropriate to talk about business.*

Another practical reason to avoid spamming is the impossibility of fulfillment. How are you going to get your product to 37 million people, or even one million, or even 50 thousand? Do you have the resources and the inventory to meet the demand? These are things to consider before posting messages to newsgroups. It is best to start with a rather small test market and see how it goes before you launch into a full scale Internet marketing campaign. When an advertisement goes out on the Internet, the company's reputation is on the line. The company will want to be sure it is able to process orders efficiently and quickly before any type of large scale Internet marketing program is put in place.

Some newsgroups absolutely do not want any sort of advertising. Users are not shy about expressing their opinions if you try to disregard their conventions, and you may be "flamed." It is easy to find out about the conventions or desires of a particular newsgroup. Most newsgroups have a list of FAQs, which will tell you what they allow and what conditions they attach to use. Of course, the *misc.forsale* groups are about selling as well as the *biz.marketplace* and *biz.misc* groups. Legitimate postings to other groups should be on-topic, hype-free, short and relevant, and perhaps point the reader to a WWW page or the *biz.misc.* area for more information. If you decide to ignore the newsgroup's conventions, be prepared for the consequences. Can you or your company afford the backlash and the damaged reputation? Only you can decide if the risk is worth it.

# Chapter 10

## Bulletin Board Systems

The big online commercial services (AOL, CompuServe, etc.) are actually nationwide bulletin board systems or "BBSs." There are also thousands of local BBSs throughout the world. Most of them are in North America, but there are also some in Japan, Europe, and South Africa. Local BBSs can be accessed by Telnet or modem on a telephone connection directly to the BBS. In order to access the information on a BBS or participate in any of its services, you must register with the BBS and then you will usually be charged an hourly fee for connect time. Most BBSs will give a potential user some free time so that they can become familiar with the BBS and "check it out." Registration consists of giving the system operator, or "sysop," your real name, address, telephone number, and choosing a nickname and/or password. To access the whole BBS, you must have a nickname or password registered with the sysop. Later, usually within the next 24 hours, the sysop will do a voice verification (that's why they need your telephone number) of all the information you gave. After that, you may need to send in other paper verification and payments if they are required. Some BBSs will let you charge your time with your credit card.

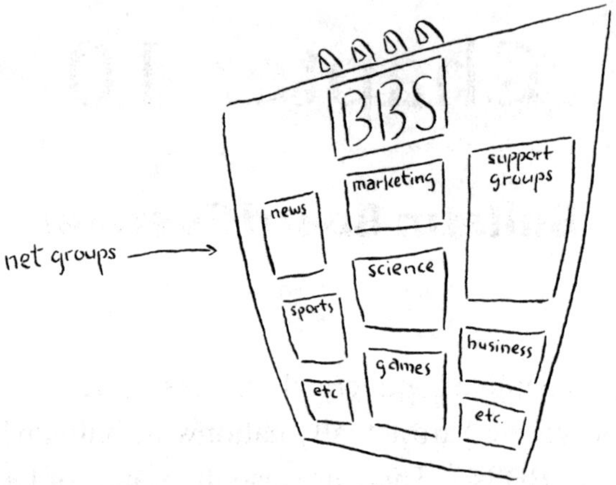


The local BBSs like to think of themselves as "entertainment social systems." Many of them have interesting names like Canned Ham, Alien's SpaceShip, Barney's Rubble, and one of the most fascinating—FlOaTIng PancReAs. They can often provide their users with access to the Internet (for an additional fee). Some of them have scads of fun features that thousands of people access every day. In BBSs you can find shareware, clip art, pictures, sounds, weather maps and forecasts, chat with local and worldwide friends, access sports connections, stocks, TV listings, movie reviews, the Daily News feed, tourism info, humor, demos, music, programming support files, matchmakers, and games.

Games are an especially hot item on the BBSs. People from all over the world play games with each other in real time. Some of the most popular are Trade Wars, Mutants, Blade Master, Galactic Empire, Shadow Realms, and Fantasy Football. You can role-play globally with people who have similar interests.

Some bulletin boards are geared to specific audiences. There are several software developers who have established their own bulletin boards to test and market their software. BBSs have become an easy way for companies to provide product improvements, updates, and debugging programs. *Bryant.com,* for example, manufactures, demonstrates, and resells software with entertainment and utility applications for other BBSs. Their software is available to registered users only. *Elysian Fields* has computer components from Galacticomm and related distributors on its BBS.

Other BBSs cater to ham radio enthusiasts, appraisers (one BBSs has an online database that is an invaluable resource for appraisers and investors), country music fans, those interested in conferencing on environmental or health issues, supporters of the arts, alternative education or politics. The bulletin board called *The Pressroom*, for example, has press schedules and transcripts, local forums on media issues, and keyword searches of White House documents. With *Online Orlando*, however, you can get feedback from WJRR radio station disk jockeys and access a 15,000 piece lyric library. Station 540 AM has a 24-hour sports station. *Online Orlando* also carries trivia games such as Trek Trivia and online role playing. *The Doctor's Office BB* has all the usual fun and games plus a 24-hour link to *The Doctor's Clinic BB* in Manassas, VA. DataCom carries a PC online catalog so that you can comparison shop for computer hardware and software. Bulletin Boards can be valuable tools for businesses if the business is targeting a local audience, has a need for high security, or wants to have a customized cyberspace presence.

If you have a very specialized product, or if you are dealing in software, you might want to create your own bulletin board. Even though they are a lot of work to maintain, your business needs may balance that out. For example, *The Flower Link* has its own bulletin board. Since there is a lot of online courting going on (see *Christie's Internet Matchmaker BB*), it makes a lot of sense to have a flower shop in a BBS. Same day flower delivery is available.

If you don't need your own bulletin board, you might want to consider advertising with some of the BBSs that have online shopping as well as other fun features. Consider your target market. If your product appeals to males under thirty years of age, the bulletin boards are a good place to market your product. BBSs can be a valuable part of a cyberspace marketing plan. (See other possible business BBSs in the appendix.)

# Section III

# The Internet Market Place

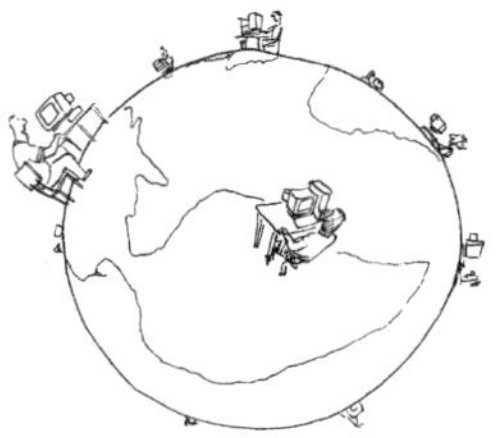

# The Internet Market Place

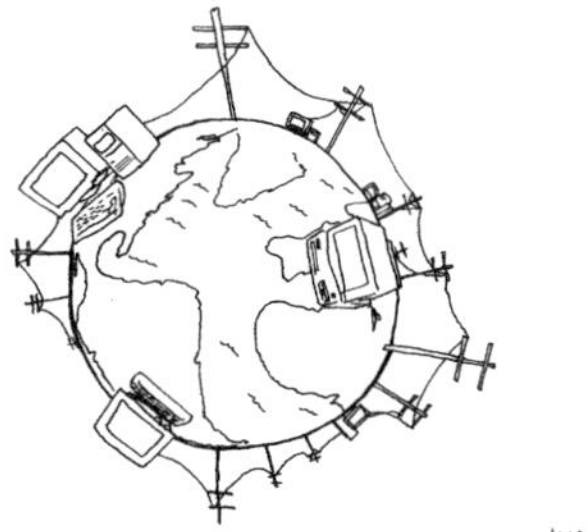

Once a business owner understands the tools and potential of the Internet, it is only a short while before he starts to see how his business could benefit by using the Internet. The benefits can't be accurately measured for most businesses. This chapter explores some of the benefits every business on the Internet should realize.

# Chapter 11

## Business Advantages of the Internet

### Cost & Time Savings

One of the best reasons for a business to use the Internet is savings. Both businesses and individuals will see big cost savings and big time savings. E-mailing your son in London, or 300 business contacts, is as cheap as calling your friend next door. It is virtually free, and it is instantaneous! Save money on long distance telephone charges, postage, and paper by using e-mail; all you pay is the cost of your monthly connection. Don't pay to fax documents again! E-mail any letter or other document for free. If your document is large or you want a color picture, computer program, or other large file to go through the Internet, "file transfer protocol" (FTP) will allow you to send immediately or make available any size document to family, friends, customers, company reps, or suppliers. FTP doesn't cost a dime more than e-mail; in fact, it doesn't cost even a dime. The Internet can also cut down on costly travel expenses, an obvious time and money waster in today's global economy. The Internet not only saves the cost of travel itself, including the airfares, hotels, etc., it will also save employee down-time in travelling. With the Internet, online meetings can replace out-of-town conferences and meetings.

Obviously, if all of the interactions traveling over the Internet are traveling at the speed of light, the savings in time is astonishing. If you e-mail your supplier in Taiwan, and he replies instantly by e-mail, how much time have you saved? How long does it take when you mail a letter to Taiwan and have to wait for a reply through the post office mail or "snail mail"? Two weeks? Three? The e-mail message travels to Taiwan, and you can receive a message back in just a few MINUTES. Just one message sent by e-mail has saved you at least two weeks. Multiply that by the number of messages you send each day, and you'll have some idea of the time that the Internet can save you. Your time savings will be enormous, whether you are corresponding with someone across town or around the world.

## Research and Development

Companies using the Internet find that they save a tremendous amount of time and money on research and development. The most striking feature of the Internet is the staggering amount of information available. It is quick and easy to use the search engines of the World Wide Web and Gopher to find and quickly gather information from colleagues, experts, and large organizations such as governments and universities located all over the world. Access databases, books, archives, pictures, research papers, repair manuals; in short, you can instantly access the collective knowledge of the world without leaving your home or office. What's more, the information is usually free.

In addition to the electronic newsletters, databases, and archives available to you on the Internet, you can "talk" to experts in many fields. Experts gather on the Internet in "chat" rooms (places on the Internet where live conversations take place) to discuss their specialties. In the chat rooms, they question each other and share research results. Is there an easier way to keep current in your field, be aware of state-of-the-art information on products, or collect new ideas from around the world? The tools of the Internet provide businesses a functional way to become more competitive with a minimum amount of investment. Many businesses use the Net as a problem solver. Instead of hiring an expensive in-house expert, employees can use the Internet to locate and speak with outside experts. Company research on every level is enhanced with little or no additional expense.

The common question is "Why would experts from around the world share their information for free?" The fact is, while experts normally don't, those who are on the Internet seem to have a different attitude. Professionals on the Internet have adopted the attitude of sharing that originally drove the Internet. The old time Internet users have a genuine fear that as businesses, with their money-grubbing attitudes, start to dominate the Internet, the attitude of sharing will disappear. The attitude of sharing is one of the neat features of the Internet! As you use the Internet, share your knowledge and perpetuate the spirit of the Internet. Yes, you can do business and make money even if you share; in fact, if you provide people on the Internet with what they want, your business will thrive.

Our friend Mary has a daughter with Turner's Syndrome. This child is missing part of her X-Y chromosome structure, and while she is of normal intelligence, she faces many problems in life. The local doctors have responded the way doctors often do. They really never explained what the problem was or what the options were. Turner's Syndrome is relatively rare, so we had never met an adult with Turner's Syndrome. We went out on the Internet and discovered several groups of people who have Turner's Syndrome and "talk" together regularly over the Internet. We "talked" to dozens of people who are living with the syndrome. We heard about their problems, successes, and personal lives.

Two pediatricians that specialize in Turner's Syndrome wrote long letters answering our questions. One of them told Mary how to make the $40,000 per year treatment costs qualify for insurance coverage. The local doctors had told her there was no way the insurance companies would pay for the treatments. Thanks to time spent on the Internet, and the help of two caring experts, her insurance company is now paying for her daughter's expensive treatments. Imagine what that means to her young family.

Why would two doctors spend their time and answer questions for free? Well, out of the hundreds of doctors that treat Turner's Syndrome, two of them on the Internet are nice guys. We can't help them, at least not today. But with their attitudes, it is probably a safe bet that they have all the business they want, and they are making a professional name for themselves in cyberspace that will surely pay dividends in day-to-day business.

## Market Research

Anyone can use the Internet to conduct market research in nontraditional ways. Businesses are investing a lot of time and money on market research because customers are becoming more demanding, and markets are becoming better defined. Market research on the Internet can be very effective because people naturally congregate in cyberspace according to their interests. Market research normally takes weeks, months, or even years using conventional research methods, and it can be very costly. The Internet makes it easy to discover and analyze the interests of any target market. Groups of people who are interested in almost any type of product or service join newsgroups by topic, and businesses can monitor their suggestions, complaints, and desires. In fact, by listening to them and addressing their concerns, businesses often come up with ideas for new products or improvements. Take a look! Whatever your business is, your target market has probably already been identified and segmented on the Internet.

## Resource Conservation

Save resources by using the Internet. Some business and government offices are urging employees to "telecommute" from their home offices in an effort to save resources and control pollution levels. Using the Internet, employees can work at home and keep in contact with co-workers and clients just as if they were at the office. Employees enjoy working from their homes, and studies show they are more productive. Businesses also improve their bottom line by not investing capital in larger offices. The telecommuting trend is bound to grow as companies realize the potential of the Internet.

Internet Relay Chat (IRC) makes it possible to carry on a live or "real time" conversation with another person or group of people on the Internet. IRC requires a specific computer "client" program that allows computers to connect to an IRC "server" computer. Those who connect to the IRC server make contact with each other by joining an IRC "channel." The names of the channels usually reflect the topics the group wants to discuss. Messages are typed and sent to the server computer which sends out all of the messages to each computer on the channel. Users are responding in real time, and the messages fly fast over the Internet. At the present time, much of the "talking" on the IRC channels is just idle conversation, but the possibility is there for some unique business applications. It is easy to have private conversations and conferences limited to invited guests. With IRC, company personnel in far flung places can conference together.

If your company requires video or audio conferencing, the Internet can actually cut the cost and meet your needs. There are computer programs, such as CU-See Me created by White Pine, and Quick Com™ by Connetix, that will let you talk over the Internet with voice communications, and the cost is about $100 for the software. It won't be long before audio and video conferencing will become a popular alternative to out-of-state or across-town meetings with associates and customers.

## Slash Advertising Costs

Businesses spend billions of dollars annually on TV, radio, magazine, and newspaper advertising. Advertising in these media is very expensive compared to advertising over the Internet. Businesses are now using every facet of the Internet to advertise and directly or indirectly sell their goods and services. However, the most popular way to advertise on the Internet is to have a Web site or full display ad on the World Wide Web. A Web site acts as a virtual store or catalog in cyberspace. Web sites have color pictures, interactive features, sound, automated ordering, and dozens of other features that bring advertising into the 21st Century. Web sites can effectively market products and services on the Internet.

Costs associated with creating and maintaining a Web site through a local access provider run between $50 and $3000 a month. Obviously, Web site costs vary widely. The exposure and effectiveness of a Web site will be greatly affected by the type of service the local access provider actually delivers. The true measure of cost is measured by the number of people reached by the advertisement. With a traditional direct mail piece, it will cost you more than $3000 in postage alone to send an advertisement to a few thousand people. The same $3000 investment in a Web site, set up with the proper links, will allow you to reach literally tens of thousands of potential customers on a daily basis every day for months.

If you decide to include your Web site in a cybermall, the cost is going to be higher than it will be if your Web site is simply maintained on a local access provider's computer, but the results will be better. Cybermalls can be compared to your local mall. Merchants congregate their stores in one location to take advantage of a collective ability to advertise and pull customers to the location. As customers come to the mall, they are exposed to all of the merchants in the mall, and the merchants benefit from the "foot traffic." Cybermalls offer merchants all of the advantages a merchant receives by becoming part of a local mall. As a result, the price of maintaining a Web site in a cybermall is higher than the price normally charged for a Web site outside of a mall.

Anyone considering setting up a commercial venture in cyberspace should look into the possibilities of associating with a cybermall. Many of the cybermalls have over 100,000 people per day come by to "window shop."

Of course, if you are going to have a Web site, there is no requirement that you have to associate with a cybermall. Many goods and services are very successfully marketed in cyberspace without any association with a mall. But, exposure to one hundred thousand people a day makes mall advertising costs incredibly low if they are considered on a per-contact basis.

## Faster and More Accurate

The Internet lets you contact your potential customers almost instantly. With your computer and a good Internet marketing campaign you can certainly reach customers faster and more efficiently than you can with a traditional direct mail campaign. Consider for a moment the time it takes to run a traditional direct mail campaign. After designing the original ad, you must take it to a printer to be printed. This process takes at least a week, if you are lucky—usually longer. Next, the ads are taken to a mail house to be stuffed and addressed. Add another week. Once the ad pieces are put in the mail, you are at the mercy of the Post Office. It is common to find bulk mail pieces that arrive over a month after they were mailed via the Post Office. First class mail generally takes two or three days to be delivered if it is mailed for delivery within the state, longer if it is out of state. The U.S. Post Office no longer guarantees that priority mail will be delivered within two days. From the time the process was begun to mail an ad until a customer receives it, there is usually a lapse of about a month to six weeks using traditional direct mail.

Publication ad campaigns, such as magazine ad campaigns, are also time intensive. Once you have designed the original ad, you must take it to an artist to be converted into camera-ready art. Next, the ad is sent to the publisher. The deadlines for ads to be submitted to a magazine are often two or three months prior to the actual publication date, so a magazine ad campaign generally takes even more time than a direct mail campaign.

Advertising over the Net need not take a lot of valuable time. The nice thing is that advertising on the Net is so simple, you can accomplish the task on your own. Even if you choose to hire someone else, the whole process can be accomplished quickly. Within a few days, a Web site can be designed and created for your business. You can create well-written electronic brochures or sales letters and send them to hundreds of interested buyers within a matter of minutes. In just minutes you can "post notices" in newsgroups in cyberspace and tell others about your product and/or direct them to your Web site on the World Wide Web. You can even prepare massive amounts of information, such as operating instructions or service manuals, and make this information available to your customers so that they can "come and get it" any time, day or night.

One of the best things about the Internet is how simple it is to update information. You can quickly and easily add or delete an item in a catalog or change a price on one of your ads. It's just as easy to correct an inaccuracy or mistake. Why is it that no matter how many times a layout is proofed there always seems to be a mistake? On the Internet, you can quickly and easily make the correction or update your information—often without any additional cost or delay.

One company put up a Web site in a cybermall for their beauty products. When the ad was placed on the Web, there was a mistake in the ad copy. The ad's guarantee said to "return the used portion" if the buyer was dissatisfied for any reason. It would obviously be very difficult to return the "used" portion of the product. Just imagine someone trying to scrape body lotion off their arms and legs to return to the seller. The owner of the company asked the mall to change the word "used" to "unused." The change was made within five minutes at no cost. What would a mistake like that cost to correct if it were made in a printed brochure? How long would it take to get a corrected copy into the customer's hands?

## Globalization - The Great Equalizer

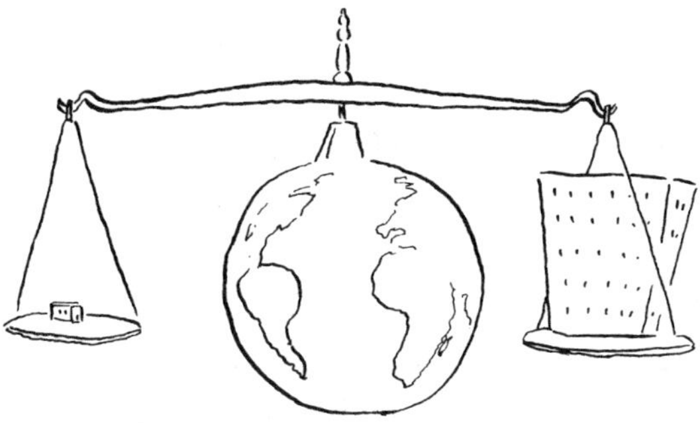

In the past, only huge multinational companies had the resources to reach a worldwide market. For the first time in history, any company can now participate in the global economy. The Internet has leveled the playing field between large and small businesses. The costs of advertising on the Internet to a worldwide market are basically the same for every business. But, the costs are minuscule compared to what the big corporations have spent historically to reach a global market. On the Internet, distances and national boundaries disappear, allowing every company to market its goods and services around the town and around the world. Businesses located in any area, no matter how remote, can compete internationally and can access information, resources, and customers that only large companies could access in the past.

Roswell James owns a bookstore in remote Nova Scotia, but his location doesn't stop him from reaching a worldwide market on the Internet. Roswell explains that everything in his business has improved since he has gone on the Net. His entire store's sales doubled the first year he started marketing using the Internet. The only thing that he did differently was set up his store on the World Wide Web and Gopher. Everyday he finds e-mail orders coming in over the Internet. He describes it as "just incredible." These orders come in from every part of the world including Europe, Australia, Japan, and many different parts of the United States. Using his database of customers from all over the world, once a month Mr. James takes about twenty minutes to transmit a four-page newsletter of new releases with specials of the month to his Internet mailing list. In his words, "This is very serious advertising, and it only costs about 65 cents total to be in communication with about 500 of my best customers."

## Company Image - Prestige

Imagine what a presence on the Internet can do for a company's image! Companies on the Internet are perceived as dynamic, progressive, on the cutting edge. Customers view them as the leaders of their respective industries. A progressive business commands respect and attention from prospective customers and competitors and that results in increased sales. The Internet provides immediate access to customers in ways that are fresh, new, and convenient. Any company using the Internet will be perceived as one which cares about its customers and is willing to use the latest technology to best serve them.

A young man in our office recently interviewed with a Japanese company that does a large amount of business in the United States. This company does not yet take advantage of the communication and information resources of the Internet. During the course of the interview, the company representative pointed out that there would be many late days spent at the office because of the ongoing need to communicate with engineers and other people in Japan involved in the manufacture of the product. Ongoing communication in this company is essential because the products are not standardized. Each product is specially made according to the customer's specifications. Imagine the time and money that could be saved if that company could communicate between the United States and Japan over the Internet! The Japanese engineers, U.S. representatives, and customers could all be included in the communications. Plans, specs, designs, contracts, and all other types of communications could be sent instantly over the Internet and be waiting 24 hours a day for review by all parties involved. No one would be left out of the information loop. Sending the messages and even holding real-time conferences on the Internet would be almost free to the company. The savings on telephone calls and faxes alone would be staggering. Design changes could be handled within minutes. Approval for projects could be given immediately.

After having worked in our office and using the Internet, the young man was astounded that the company did not have an Internet connection. It was hard for him to believe that an otherwise technically advanced company, so dependent on research and ongoing overseas communication, wasn't connected. This point alone caused him to perceive the company as behind the times. Of course, every company wants to have a public image as a progressive company. A business on the Internet cultivates a progressive image for your company and it will pay dividends.

## Improve Customer Support

Many consumers miss the "personal touch" selling that has been all but eliminated from traditional specialty stores. Today's retail marketing has moved to high-volume discount stores with little or no "personal touch" customer relations. The prices may be lower, but shoppers complain that store clerks are rude, hard to find, and know little or nothing about the products they sell. Cybershopping is bringing new joy to shopping. Consumers enjoy shopping on the Internet from the privacy and comfort of their own homes, where they can "browse" at their leisure. Yet, they are able to communicate quickly with a human if they want further details, a different size, or special handling. Using the Internet in your business, you will be able to provide the kind of support that customers yearn for and that will keep them coming back.

When it comes to closing the distance between themselves and the customer while improving customer service, Federal Express is setting the pace. Federal

Express is the world's largest express transportation company. They deliver 2.2 million items to 192 countries each working day. Not only is Federal Express the largest parcel delivery service in the world, they are the technology leaders in the express carrier industry. Federal Express was the first to install computers in vans, provide sophisticated automation in the mail room, and develop tracking software. Federal Express has always done its best to be in the forefront of the business world and apply the newest technology to their express delivery service. They were quick to apply the Internet to their shipping service.

In January 1995, Dennis Jones, chief information officer at Federal Express, said "We're leading the industry down the information superhighway. Last month almost 70% of our volume originated through automated technologies. With the general availability of *FedEx Ship* and our Internet presence, we're confident about reaching our goal of conducting nearly 100% of our business online."

In an effort to achieve this goal, Federal Express has set up a World Wide Web site on the Internet *(http://www.FedEx.com)*. This Web site provides users with up-to-date news and information about Federal Express services and allows them to track the status of their shipments. They also make available *FedEx Ship*, their downloadable, free desk-top shipping software. This software allows customers with personal computers, modems, and laser printers to generate shipping documents and maintain a shipping history.

## The Way of the Future

The Internet is the best way for businesses to capitalize on the market of the future. It is undeniable that values are shifting and lifestyles are changing. The Internet is the logical tool that businesses can use to adapt to the consumer's changing wants and needs. The competitive advantage associated with being a large and diversified company is shrinking. However, the competitive advantage associated with the ability to cut costs and reach unexplored markets by using the tools of the Internet is there for all. The companies and businesses that connect to the Internet today will be the ones that have a competitive advantage tomorrow.

# Chapter 12

## Understanding Cyberspace Culture

### The Dark Side

Thus far we have been talking about the "ideal" Internet community, but the Internet has its unpleasant facets as well. There are a few people on the Internet who would take advantage of its trusting environment. Keep in mind that the "friendly" person on the other end of your Internet communication is a stranger, and you need to treat him like a stranger. Because you can't see him, hear the tone in his voice, or get any feel for his physical presence, you need to treat a stranger on the Internet with even more caution than you would treat a stranger you meet on the street. Be wary about giving personal details about yourself to anyone online. Educate your children to never give out personal information about themselves or anyone else. Your children should certainly never agree to meet with someone who contacts them on the Net. Your children need to know that. You need to teach them.

## Pornography

Even the most rabid anti-regulation activist would have to admit that there *is* pornography on the Net. A famous, but now largely discredited article in *Time* magazine, left the impression that as much as 80 per cent of the content on the Internet was pornographic. Marty Rimm's study, on which the article was based, actually found that only 3 percent of the *newsgroups'* messages are pornographic images. And, it should be pointed out that the images in the newsgroups are in binary form. Nobody can just stumble upon them accidentally. Whoever wants to view them has to know where they are, how to download them, and how to decode them to be viewed. Special software is required in order to view the decoded pictures.

A student in a very conservative university was suspended for downloading pornographic materials from newsgroups. His defense was that he did not know what the material was before he downloaded it. He stated, "It was just a small file that looked interesting. I had no idea what it was when I downloaded it." Not likely. The sites with erotic pictures are clearly labeled and often include explicit descriptions of their images and even warnings to those who want to download them.

What about Web sites that contain porn? On the Web, it is fairly easy to access sexually explicit material, if you are looking for it. Most of the Web sites that contain pornography have a disclaimer on their Web site and ask that you verify that you are over 18 before they let you in. But, it is easy to say you are over 18. All you have to do is click on "yes" or "continue." If you have a home-based business and want to make sure your children aren't using your computer to joyride through the red-light district, or if you want to reduce employee access to sexually explicit material, there are several software programs available that block sites which contain erotic material. The average retail price is around $50. Look at: SurfWatch *(http://www.surfwatch.com)*, Net Nanny *(http://www.netnanny.com/netnanny)*, and CyberPatrol *(http://www.microsys.com/cyber)*.

## Scams

Legitimate businesses don't use the anonymity inherent on the Internet to defraud customers. But, there are unscrupulous individuals who use classified ads, bulletin board notices, newsgroup discussions, and even Web sites to promote shady deals.

A young man recently offered computer equipment for sale over the Internet. Within a couple of weeks he had made tens of thousands of dollars in sales. You guessed it, he didn't actually have any computer equipment to sell. The local police got to him very fast, and even as a minor, he is now doing time for his "computer sales."

The same sort of warnings that you would hear in the real world apply on the Internet. The saying, "If it sounds too good to be true, it probably is," is very valid on the Internet. Watch out for exaggerated and unsubstantiated promises of instant wealth, and don't make them yourself. The Net crowd is terribly suspicious of get-rich-quick schemes, and they're not afraid to express their annoyance with such phony claims. You can also check out businesses with the Better Business Bureau (800-876-7060) or go to its Web site *(http://www.bbb.org)*. The Federal Trade Commission also maintains a Web site *(http://www.ftc.gov)* with helpful tips for uncovering scams on the Internet.

## Netiquette

Netiquette is the set of "socially accepted" rules that govern Internet interactions. In the early days of the Internet, the Netiquette rules were very strict, and any type of business activity on the Net was a violation of the rules. Basically, the computer and scientific types governed the Net by their own rules. If they were unhappy with an action, they let it be known.

Some of the rules netters chose to enforce were interesting and inconsistent. For instance, pornography and get-rich-quick scams were posted all over the Internet, and no one batted an eye. But if someone tried to sell his new software program, he was flamed mercilessly. One Internet enthusiast described the Net as the only true anarchy because the rules depended on which self-appointed guardian you happened to run into in cyberspace.

## Flaming

There are some socially challenged folks on the Internet who delight in causing controversy in newsgroups. They love "flaming" their victims by sending extremely rude, insulting and often vulgar e-mail replies. They act as self-appointed cyberpolice and attempt to enforce their own interpretation of what is appropriate on the Net.

Some have likened the Internet culture to the early days of the Wild West—uncivilized and lawless. It does help to be somewhat thick-skinned as you get to know your way around the Internet, particularly in the newsgroups and listservs. Sometimes the exchanges sound like teenagers' conversations. Netters may say insulting things to each other and be extremely blunt, but usually no one takes offense. Flamers, on the other hand, hide behind the anonymity of their screen names and let their uncensored venom spew. Newbies (the name given to new users of the Internet) are often the targets of the flaming. That's why it's a good idea to "lurk" or just observe for a couple of weeks before plunging into conversations on the Net. You'll soon get a feel for it.

## Viruses

You don't need to spend a lot of time and money worrying about viruses, i.e., those computer programs designed to destroy data or otherwise disrupt your computer system. Viruses can only infect a computer system if they are contained in information "downloaded" over the Internet or by putting an infected disk into the computer. The chances of getting a virus by participating in newsgroups or surfing the World Wide Web and looking at Web sites are just about zero. Pictures and information files downloaded over the Internet very seldom carry viruses. The biggest chance of getting a virus in your system comes when you download an "executable" file, such as a computer program or game.

The best protection against viruses is to run an anti-virus program every time the system starts up and to check every foreign disk you put into the system. The commercially available anti-virus programs are good, but they do have to be updated regularly because new viruses are being developed every day.

Try to download files only from reputable Internet sites. To see if a site is reputable, just find out how long it has been up on the Internet. Sites that distribute viruses don't stay in business long before their deeds are discovered and the word gets out.

# Chapter 13

## Internet Security

### Credit Cards and Net Security

One of the impediments to business blossoming on the Internet is people's reluctance to send credit card numbers over the Net. Sending a credit card number over the Internet to a legitimate business is not much riskier than giving it over the telephone or writing it on an order form. According to Forrester Research, the approximate fraud rate for every $1000 billed is only $1 on the Internet. Compare that to $1.41 for MasterCard and $16.00 for telephone calling cards. "An important thing to remember is that your liability is limited to a maximum of $50 as long as fraudulent charges are reported within 60 days." (Kiplinger's Personal Finance Magazine, January 1996) However, when a credit card number is given at an unsecured Internet site, there is a small security risk. The card holder doesn't know exactly how the card details will reach the merchant. The information will pass through multiple computers before it reaches its final destination. It is possible that someone along the way could intercept the card details and use the information illegally. The chances of this happening are very unlikely, but it does happen. To help consumers be comfortable dealing on the Internet, merchants should use "secured" server sites or use a reputable cybermall which has "secured" order forms.

How can you tell a secure site? On Web sites viewed using Netscape, there is a key in the bottom left-hand corner of the screen. If the key has a break in the middle of it, the connection is not secure. The messages traveling to the connection are not encrypted or scrambled to prevent unauthorized access. If the key is whole, then the server is secure. Some cybermalls have secure servers so that buyers will feel comfortable about ordering and paying online. Some sites post a message notifying the shopper that he is entering a secure area. Most Web browsers now include a similar feature.

NetCheque is an accounting server which allows registered users to write electronic checks to other users. These checks may be sent through e-mail. After deposit, the check authorizes transfer of account balances from one user's account to another, just the same as in your home town bank when a paper check is used. More information about the NetCheque system is available at *http://www.netcheque.org/info/netcheque.*

Several companies have developed software to make it possible to use credit cards over the Internet without the credit card information being stored on the business' Web site. When the credit card information isn't "stored" by the merchant on the Internet, it becomes even harder for unauthorized users to get at it. CheckFree Wallet™, for example, offers its easy software program free at its site: (*http://www.mc2-csr.com/vmall/checkfree/v20/software.html.)*

After downloading the program, you connect to CheckFree and register yourself and the credit cards you plan to use. Of course, the system works only with businesses that have embraced it.

## Encryption

Software programs that encrypt messages are available. Encryption is a process that codes details, such as a credit card number or other private information, so that the details can only be read by those who have the decoder corresponding to the program originally used to encrypt the information. Attorneys and big corporations which have a need to transmit sensitive and/or confidential documents often use an encryption program called Pretty Good Privacy (PGP). With PGP, the encrypted message can only be read by a person who has a special decryption key, and it is safe to assume no one can "decrypt" the message except the addressee. PGP uses a two-key type of encryption: a private key which is never given out to anyone and a public key which is freely given to others. People who send you messages use your public key, and you use your private key to decrypt them. Only you can decode your encrypted mail with your private key—it is very secure. Obviously, the people with whom you correspond will need to have PGP programs running on their computers.

PGP is available at the MIT site *(http://web.mit.edu/network/pgp-form.html)*. You can fill out the forms online for permission to download the program. It's free, but there are licensing agreements that you must read and agree to.

## Digital Signatures

The latest development in making secure transactions on the Internet is the use of digital signatures, a sort of electronic identification card. As the Internet develops as a universal business medium, digital signatures will be used to verify the senders and receivers of confidential information. A digital certificate is attached to a user's public key. The certificate can then be "looked up" to verify the sender is who they say they are. It is hoped and expected that digital signatures will become recognized by governments as legal and binding in order to transmit legal contracts over the Net. Utah and California were the first two states to recognize digital signatures as legal signatures, but other states have laws pending. *Entrust 2.0*, software produced by Northern Telecom, creates and manages digital signatures for businesses. Costs for a business can be reduced if its employees can use digital identification to transfer sensitive documents, authorize purchase orders, and execute other transactions.

Obviously, the Internet is in a rapid transition phase trying to improve security and make merchants and consumers safe in cyberspace. Futurists at Jupiter Communications estimate that by the year 2000, the online marketplace will be handling $7.2 billion worth of commerce. They predict $4.5 billion of that will be on the Web. Some predictions estimate a lot more than $7.2 billion in business will be transacted over the Internet by the year 2000. Whatever the amount will be, companies like VeriFone, Inc., which handles the majority of credit card payments in the real world, are teaming up with Netscape to provide secure financial payment systems in cyberspace. Soon the whole operation of a business on the Internet will be seamless and secure.

## Hackers

What about hackers? The typical home user would probably not be the target of an attack on his or her system. The risk increases when valuable or classified information is stored on the computer and the computer is continually connected to the Internet, as is common in large companies. With a SLIP or PPP connection (the type of connection found in almost all home and small business connections), the files on the computer would only be at risk when the computer is actually in use and connected to the Internet. Even when a single-user computer is in use, it is nearly impossible for a hacker to come to the computer and cause trouble. If you are ever using your computer on the Internet and you feel like you have lost control, or the hard disk drive starts to work hard in an unexplained manner, simply hit the off switch on the computer and start again. It is unlikely that a hacker was playing with your computer, but the off switch is an easy solution to any unexplained action of your computer while it is on the Internet, so don't be afraid to hit the switch.

If a computer is off or it is not hooked to the Internet, some other type of network, or a telephone modem hookup, it is completely safe from hackers.

Computers that are left on, hooked into the Internet, or that can be accessed remotely using a telephone hookup, are exposed to hackers. Their owners need to take precautions. Elaborate software (firewall software) is available to protect such computers from hackers.

# Section IV

# Internet Business Checklist

# Internet Business Checklist

By now you realize that whether your business is big or small, you will benefit by using the Internet. Communication is not only cheaper and faster, it is also more complete because graphics and sound can be included in any message. These enhanced capabilities mean that if you advertise on the Internet, sales will increase. Actually, your business doesn't have to be "on" the Internet to successfully advertise on the Internet. You can hire someone to create your Internet ad and then use a remote computer, one that is outside of your company, to store your advertisement and make the ad available or "serve" the ad to the public over the Internet. The computer used to "serve" the ad to the Internet public is called a "server."

Even though you can hire someone else and use a server to put your advertisements on the Internet, it is really better to actually use the Internet yourself to establish a presence in Cyberspace. The following checklist gives a complete outline of the items you need to consider in order to use the Internet.

## 1. Get an Internet connection

An Internet connection requires either a PPP (Point to Point Protocol) or a SLIP (Serial Line Internet Protocol) connection so that you can access the Internet directly. PPP and SLIP are the connection "rules" or technical standards that permit a computer full Internet access using a normal telephone line connection. This sounds scary but actually it is easy; just find an Internet provider (ISP), and your provider will give you software with the appropriate connection information. You don't need to worry about the technical aspects of your connection.

A local ISP is usually the cheapest way to connect to the Internet. To find a local provider, look in the computer section of your newspaper, visit your local computer store, or call the computer science department at your local college or university. Call a couple of these local access providers and find one that will connect you to the Internet using a local telephone number and give you a software package that you can easily install. ISPs should charge you no more than $20 to $30 a month for a single user with unlimited Internet access time. The access provider should also provide you with storage space for your Web site and any FTP files you want to make available. There may be an additional charge for the Web site storage and FTP file storage, but it shouldn't be much. Shop around to get the best deal possible. Watch for hidden costs. Businesses connecting to the Internet are charged according to the possible number of simultaneous users, the number of e-mail addresses needed, and the amount of computer storage space required.

There are a couple of national Internet Access Providers. They have advantages over the guy down the street that sets up shop and has a computer and a dozen modems in his garage. The biggest advantage is nationwide access using local telephone numbers. When traveling, you can use the national access provider number anywhere and work on the Internet with no additional telephone charges or service charges. You can access the Internet from any location and it is just as if you were sitting in your home or office.

## 2. Pick a domain name

Choosing a domain name is purely optional. Most people and businesses never have their own unique domain name. However, a unique domain name gives you a strong identity in cyberspace. You can pick an identity that mirrors your real life identity, or your cyberspace identity can be totally new. A domain name should be unique and easy for people to remember and associate with you and/or your products. A domain name will become part of your e-mail address and your Web site's URL.

A domain name must be registered with InterNIC. Contact InterNIC at *http://www.internic.net* or (619) 455-4600. At the present time, it costs US$100 to register a domain. Registration is good for two years, after which it will need to be renewed. Your access provider can register your domain name. By using a local provider to register your domain name, you won't have to worry about any of the paperwork, and your domain name will be set up for easy connection. Domain names can be moved from ISP to ISP, so don't worry if you want to change your Internet provider later. It is important to register your domain name ASAP, because the good domain names are going fast.

### 3. Establish an e-mail address

A local or national access provider assigns your e-mail addresses once an account is established with their service. If you don't get your own domain name, your address will simply include part of your ISP's address. If you have a business, it is a good idea to make your domain name part of the address. It may cost a little more to have your business domain name carried on the provider's computers as part of your e-mail address, but it is worth the cost to establish a strong presence in cyberspace. Once you have your own address or are satisfied with your provider, start using your e-mail address on all of your business cards, letterhead, invoices, and other printed business materials.

Note that if your provider can arrange your address so that the address has a user's portion and then only your domain name (i.e., *lee@infodirect.com*), your e-mail address can be moved to another provider and the public will never know it has been moved. However, if the e-mail address contains part of the provider's domain name (i.e., *lee@infodirect.itsnet.com*), you cannot change providers without changing the e-mail address and all of your printed materials.

### 4. Develop a unique signature file

At the end of e-mail letters and newsgroup postings, a "signature file" can be added. Signature files are the cyberspace version of a logo on printed letterhead. However, they are presented at the end of the message rather than on the top of the page where a logo normally appears. The signature file or "block" usually has your e-mail address, fax number, and maybe your snail mail address and telephone number. Of course the company name and slogan could be included in a business signature file. A personal signature file often contains a cute saying or thought. Be creative, and put across your message using your signature file. It isn't necessary to have a signature file attached to your correspondence, but it is a nice idea. And, it can make your Internet communications stand out.

## 5. Become comfortable with the Internet

Becoming comfortable with the Internet is easier said than done. Actually, even getting connected can be a scary experience for someone who isn't comfortable with a computer.

Getting our office and each of our own computers hooked onto the Internet was a frustrating experience. We wanted to get hooked up to the Internet in mid-1994, so we bought dozens of books at the bookstores. Some of the books we only waded through the first thirty pages before we discarded them. We even read a number of them cover to cover, but we weren't any closer to getting on the Internet. We got mad and decided to become comfortable on the Internet by doing whatever it took. It took a lot of time and thousands of dollars, because we signed up for every one of the training programs we could find. Most of the training turned out to be a waste also, but we finally learned.

As a result of our frustrating experience, we developed a complete "how-to" self-taught training course that walks the user through the experience all of the way, from buying a computer to doing Telnet and FTP. The course is called *WorldWalk*™. It has two fifty minute videos and six workbooks that explain each feature of the Internet in easy-to-understand language. They give you the chance to "look over our shoulder" as we demonstrate each part of the Internet.

Most people hopping on the Internet today go directly to the World Wide Web, which is the fun, colorful, glitzy part of the Internet. However, it is only a part of the Internet. Tools such as Gopher, Usenet, FTP, IRC Chat, Telnet, and others are important to doing business in cyberspace. It is best to become comfortable with each facet of the Internet. Our how-to step-by-step tutorial on the Internet, *WorldWalk*™*,* covers each Internet tool. It's fun! You can order a copy at 1-800-WANT-NET (1-800-926-8638). If you haven't started on the Internet or you are frustrated with the whole experience, it will help. Don't give up!

## 6. Creating an interesting Web site

A Web site is a good idea for advertising. If your access provider allows it, list your Web site under your domain name. In this way, you'll have a Web address that will be easily remembered and simple. The most successful Web sites are attractive, informative, and interactive. Load your Web site and **announce it in the right places**. Look at Appendix 2 for the right places. Consider putting your Web site in a cybermall.

## 7. Be prepared...

to answer your e-mail inquiries with a well-prepared sales letter,
to take and fill orders,
to interact with customers.

# Chapter 14

## Getting Connected

To get on the Internet, you'll need to have a computer, a modem, a phone line, software, and access to the Internet. Older computers can be used to access the Internet, but they are so slow that the Internet becomes more of a chore than the joy it should be. Ideally, you'll want a 486 megahertz or faster computer. You'll need to be running Windows or another graphical type of software. The actual software you need to connect to the Internet and "surf" cyberspace will be provided to you by the company that provides you with access to the Internet. This company will be considered either an "access provider" or an "online service." Each company has its own software which allows your computer to "talk" to their computer and gain access to the worldwide network of computers on the Internet. You will receive the software from the company as part of your "start-up package."

In order for your computer to "talk" to the provider's computer, a modem must be used with your computer. You need a modem and the provider also needs a modem. The modem controls the speed at which data flow into your computer (usually in bits per second, referred to as "baud"). You want a fast modem. If you already have a 14,400 baud modem, that is sufficient; anything slower will cause you nothing but frustration. You may actually save money if you get a faster modem, such as 28,800 or 33,600 baud, because you can do your business over the Internet much faster, and your connection time will be shorter. Most newer computers already have a modem built into them. Make sure you need one before you go shopping.

You don't need a special phone line to handle your Internet connection. The regular line into your home or office works great. However, when your computer is accessing the Internet, the telephone line is tied up, and nobody can call in or out over the line. Because the Internet is such a valuable resource and a lot of fun, ideally you'll install another telephone line directly to your computer.

There are a variety of ways to obtain access to the Internet. Each one has advantages and disadvantages. They vary widely in regard to cost, services provided, and flexibility. The three main types of Internet access are:

1. **Online Commercial Services**, such as CompuServe, AOL, GEnie, and Prodigy
2. **National Access Providers**, such as NetCom, Unidial, and PSI
3. **Local Access Providers**

## Online Commercial Services

Often the first exposure to the Internet is with one of the large, fee-based commercial services such as America Online, Prodigy, GEnie or CompuServe. These companies have established local telephone connections so that almost anyone can reach them by calling a local telephone number. When you dial in using one of their telephone numbers, your computer connects to the massive computers maintained by the company. These services do not automatically connect you to the Internet. In fact, many people who use one of the online services never connect to the Internet. The massive computers, owned and controlled by the online service companies, have tons of information, let you send e-mail (even to someone on the Internet), get stock quotes, chat, and do dozens of other things. But, you are not on the Internet. The online services will let you have access to the Internet through their computers, but you should note that the access they give you to the Internet is controlled access. That means you only get to use the parts of the Internet they let you use.

Historically, the online services have been easy to use, while the Internet has been complicated to use. The Internet is so dynamic and so vast that it has been very intimidating to the public in general. The online services provided all of the software, good support (well OK, some type of support), and everything was nicely organized and presented in the online service's computers. Since late 1995, software has been developed that makes the Internet as easy to use as the online services. Oh, the Internet is still vast and everything isn't all organized for you, but there is no reason to be intimidated. The information available to you on the Internet is many, many, many times greater than the information on all the online service companies' computers combined.

The big online services certainly have their place and they can be a very valuable resource, but one of the biggest disadvantages to using the online services as of this writing, is that they can also be very expensive. If you only spent 1 hour a day using the Internet on an online service, it could cost you $75 a month. (However, perhaps even by the time you read this, most of the major online service companies will be forced to move to a pricing structure similar to [and competitive with] the national and local access providers.) A local access provider should give you basically unlimited use of the Internet itself for between $20 and $30 per month. Each service has unique features. Many people find full satisfaction using an online service, but if you are really going to surf the Internet, you should consider using a local access provider to get you on the Internet. Local access providers are discussed in the next section.

---

***Marketing Tip:*** *The online services can be great marketing tools. Millions of people use the online services regularly. You should consider maintaining a basic online service account to at least monitor marketing activities on the service. You should note that the average person using the online services buys more goods and services over the online service than the average person using the Internet buys over the Internet. That doesn't mean you should discount the Internet in any way. The Internet is still a great market because there are a lot more people surfing the Internet than there are using the online services. Yes, the* *number of people using the online services is large, but the number of people using the Internet is mind boggling. In addition to an online account, you should also consider maintaining a local access provider account to connect you into the Internet and give you unlimited time to market, surf, or do whatever you want in cyberspace.*

Following is a list of the major online service providers and the easiest way to get to them. Of course, the online service industry changes every day, so don't be surprised if things are different:

**America Online®** (AOL) 800-227-6364. Check out their Small Business Center; it is a good service.

**CompuServe®** 800-848-8199. CompuServe can be very useful for research, but they'll charge you for each article you retrieve from their computers. Many of the "with-it" businesses have had accounts on CompuServe since the early 1980s. The forums, which are special areas on CompuServe, are good places to find contacts and/or clients.

**Prodigy®** 800-776-3449. There are fees for use of many of the neat parts of the Prodigy services. Prodigy has good classified ads and their business areas are certainly worth checking out.

**Microsoft Network®** 800-386-5550. Microsoft has included Internet access capability as part of their Windows 95 package. Naturally, Microsoft would like you to use their connection to the Internet, and you can choose this option with the click of a button. If you already have an local Internet access provider, you can continue using that service by configuring your connection through a series of menus within Windows 95.

## National Providers

**NetCom** (800-501-8649) and **UniDial** (800-211-9683) are considered "national providers." They are large companies that have established local access numbers around the United States, Canada, and other countries. By calling the local number in your area, you can have a direct access to the Internet. The national providers do not maintain their own huge databases and do not try to control your activities in cyberspace as the online services do. They simply use their system to give you direct access to the Internet.

National providers give you access to the Internet a lot cheaper than the online services, but they don't have the well-organized information and services that the online services provide. In some areas, the national providers don't have local dialing numbers for your computer to call. Because they don't have a local number, they will give you an 800 number which isn't really a free call. If your only access is through an 800 number you will pay an extra fee for access, and you will spend a fortune real fast trying to play on the Net. However, the 800 number access is nice for people who travel and want to make sure they can easily access the Internet to communicate, check e-mail, and do other Internet activities that don't use up a lot of time. The number of local access telephone numbers is growing very quickly, so even if the national provider didn't have a local number for you last time you checked, they may have a local number for you today.

## Local Access Providers

Local access providers are usually people in your own community who have spent money on hardware, software, and phone lines so that you and others can find their way onto the Internet without investing a fortune in special computer equipment or becoming a computer genius.

The connection that a typical consumer or small business will want to get is either a SLIP (Serial Line Internet Protocol) connection or a PPP (Point-to-Point) connection from an ISP. These connections give your computer direct access to the Internet over regular phone lines. They are different from shell or dial-up accounts, which also use regular phone lines, but which offer indirect access by allowing you to use the Internet through the operation of a remote computer, such as a school's or a company's computer.

Local providers typically charge around $20 a month and give you from 40 to 50 hours of free monthly access. Time beyond your free hours is charged at an hourly rate and is usually substantially cheaper than the major online services. Some providers charge a flat monthly rate for unlimited use. Check around for the best deal with the features that you need. To find a provider in your area, look in the classified ads under "computers," drop by computer stores and ask who they'd recommend, or if you know someone with Internet access, ask them. If you know someone with access, you may also wish to visit the

Celestin site *(http://www.celestin.com/pocia/),* which has a list of providers. Many ISPs are listed there as both local and national providers. The local ones are sorted by zip code. You can also download this file by ftp *(ftp.pcnet.com subdirectory/users/dpg/ftp/list-of-access-providers.txt)*

Here are some things to consider when shopping for a local access provider:

- **What Internet features does the provider support? (E-mail? FTP? World Wide Web? Newsgroups? etc.)**
- **What kind of software package is included with your connection? (Netscape?)**
- **Does the provider have any restrictions regarding business use?**
- **How much online time are you allowed every month? Is it a flat rate or is there a per hour charge?**
- **Will the provider be available for technical support?**
- **How much would it cost (up front and per month) to keep a Web site on the World Wide Web on the provider's system?**
- **Does the provider have FTP space?**
- **How often could you expect to get a busy signal when you sign on?**

When you talk to your provider, you may only want a single user's account that provides one e-mail address. A commercial account that provides up to five e-mail addresses will require an additional investment. Such accounts allow you to send and receive e-mail at different addresses. This can be very helpful in tracking sales, keeping your private correspondence separate from your business accounts, sorting out multiple users in your office, etc. If you have several different projects going on and you need to keep them divided, you can use the several e-mail addresses to separate them. If you don't mind all the e-mail going into one box, a single e-mail account is fine.

***Helpful Tip:*** *Your local provider will ask you to pick a password to protect unauthorized access to your account and your mail. Pick a mixture of letters and numbers, capitals and lower case letters. It should be something you can remember, yet not so obvious that anyone could figure it out. One way to pick a password is to think of a simple sentence with words and numbers and take the first letter of each word in the sentence. For example, "Carla's car is Red with 2 green stripes" would result in the password: CciRw2gs.*

## Virtual Servers

In addition to having a reliable Internet connection, you may also want to consider having a virtual server. With this option, you rent Web space from a local provider that has the computer power to make you look like your own server. This allows you to use your own domain name without using any part of the provider's domain name (see Chapter 15 on how to get a domain name). Some of the big servers have full-blown Web site construction teams to help you set up a custom site. The main advantage gained by using a virtual server lies in having a Web address that's practical and easy to remember. It's yours and it makes you look like a real Internet player.

Compare our old Web address:

*http://www.infodirect.com/infodirect/ww.html*

to our new one:

*http://worldwalk.com*

It's a lot easier to get the new one on the business cards and letterhead! It is a lot cheaper to have a virtual server set up than it is to become your own provider.

## Becoming Your Own Provider

If your business is large enough to warrant it, you may wish to consider becoming your own provider, but it does require a large investment in money, knowledge, and time. This method of getting onto the Internet also requires a commitment to the continual maintenance of a computer system. Costs associated with setting up a system like this will vary somewhere between $35,000 and $250,000, depending on your hardware needs. Becoming a provider will also require that a T1 or a T3 telephone line be installed which will cost about $1,000 per month.

# Chapter 15

## Choose and Register a Domain Name

Choosing and registering a domain name is an essential step for businesses that want a serious presence on the Internet. Most businesses try to use their business name and trademarks on the Internet. If you already have a business or are thinking of starting one, in cyberspace or the real world, it makes sense to protect your trademarks and trade names before exposing them to the public. A trademark, tradename or servicemark is any symbol, word, name or device used by a company to identify its goods or services. Traditionally a trademark becomes the source of recognition for your company's goods and services, while a tradename is the name of the company. Once issued, both trademarks and tradenames are protected indefinitely under state, federal and common law.

Trademark ownership is quite easy to establish. A company must first use the symbol they wish to trademark, then register it with the Patent and Trademark Office (PTO) of the Federal Government. It is wise to perform a trademark search before using a symbol, in order to make certain it is not already in use. To claim a trademark, simply find a unique symbol and affix the little "TM" to the mark whenever it is used. The "TM" provides notice to others of your ownership and the right you are claiming to use the trademark. Registration with the PTO is not necessary to use the "TM" notice, but registration expands your rights and gives the world "official" notice of your claimed rights.

A trademark can be obtained by filing an application, with a processing fee, and a sample of the "mark," at the Patent and Trademark Office, Public Service Center, Washington DC 20231. Once a Federal registration is issued, the registrant may give notice of registration by using the ® symbol or the phrase "Registered in U.S. Patent and Trademark Office." The ® registration symbol may not lawfully be used prior to complete registration. However, the trademark owners may use a ™ (trademark) or SM (servicemark) symbol to indicate a claim of ownership while waiting for the Federal trademark registration.

If you don't have a trademarked name and don't really want to go to all the trouble and expense of trademarking a name, you can still do business on the Internet by selecting an unclaimed domain name. It is easy to check whether a name is available on the Internet. Simply ask your access provider to find out whether or not a name is already being used. It's a good idea to have four or five names in mind because a lot of domain names have already been claimed.

It is not necessary to use your name or your company's name as your domain name. For example, the travel agency, Executive Travel Services, wants to use their Web site to promote their travel packages. Their theme is "Unlimited Sunsets," which conjures up an image of endless glamorous destinations—the hold-your-breath kind that inspire you to take pictures of glorious sunsets. When they chose a domain name, they wanted one that would be easy to remember and also trigger a vision of the kind of travel programs they provide. They chose "sunsets.com". It's easy to remember, and it's tied in visually with the stunning picture that welcomes a visitor to their Web site.

To register a domain name, go to the InterNIC Web site *(http://rs.internic.net/reg/reg-forms.html)* and follow the instructions. Hyperlinks are provided so you can easily move between the form and the instructions if you need help. The name can be registered electronically over the Internet at the Network Solutions Website, and then you can pay for the registration by postal mail. The initial cost for a domain name is $100 which will activate the domain name for two years. Thereafter, the charge is $50 a year.

# Chapter 16

## Creating a Web Site

### A Good Web Site

Many who cruise the Web daily do so simply to entertain themselves because sightseeing on the World Wide Web is fun. With literally millions of Web addresses in the world, ingenuity is needed to draw consumers to a particular site. Creative graphics enhance Web sites, but they are not the only things attracting Web travelers. Valuable information, attractive prices unavailable anywhere else, products that are in demand, prizes and contests, interaction with others—these things are what Web travelers are looking for.

### Search Engines

A great way to increase the visibility of a Web site is to register it with search engines on the Net. Search engines are like online electronic yellow pages. Internet users looking for products or information rely on search engines like Yahoo and Lycos to direct them to the right place. The users enter the subjects they are looking for, and the engines match the request to registered sites and supply the Internet addresses. Many search engine registration services are free and offer an enhanced marketing opportunity for you.

Submitting information to the search engine services is not hard to do, but it does take a little time (an hour or two once you get the routine down). You need the URL of your Web site, a short 25-word description of the site, plus 5 to 10 keywords that potential customers might use to search the Net. You'll also need the usual name, address, telephone number, contact name and e-mail address. With this information, go to the Submit-it Web site (*http://www.submit-it.com*). Complete instructions are online for submitting the name and URL of the site to many search engines. You can do it all at this site.

# Chapter 17

## Processing an Internet Sale

### Fulfillment

An essential ingredient of any marketing program is fulfillment. Fulfillment means "to promptly carry out, accomplish or satisfy promised conditions." From a marketing standpoint, fulfillment has a deeper meaning—"to strengthen a company's market." Good fulfillment means satisfied customers, strengthened business reputation, and increased profitability. The Internet can really help improve company fulfillment by speeding delivery time and thereby increasing customer satisfaction. Customers can order products over the Net and the orders will be fed directly into the company's computer database allowing instant processing. Be sure you have product ready to ship when you begin your online marketing. And you'll need to have the personnel to handle the orders whether you do it yourself or hire a fulfillment house.

## Payment

It is important to decide how to handle payment for goods and services ordered over the Internet. Marketing experts have found that in traditional marketing there is generally better response when a company fills the order and then bills. These experts admit that there is a sizable risk from customers who do not pay, but the sales benefits often outweigh the loss. Internet marketing, however requires prepayment. In a global market it is almost impossible to follow-up in a cost-effective manner, and you'll have a difficult time enforcing payment. If you're selling a small-ticket item or two in a newsgroup or in a classified ad, always ask for payment by money order or cashier's check. Depending on the item, perhaps you'll even be able to send it COD.

On a Web site there are several options for payment. Certainly the buyer can send a check or money order to the company, and the product will be shipped out. If the company is not well known, then customers might be reluctant to order this way, and some of the benefits of Internet shopping are lost. You want to make it as easy as possible to order your product. If your business can accept and process credit card orders, include a phone or fax number where you can be contacted. Perhaps you have a toll-free number for orders. Products can also be ordered online at the click of a button. The buyer is then given a choice of payment options. He enters his credit card number, verifies the purchase, and the order is sent to your e-mail address for you to process.

## Merchant Accounts

Processing credit cards requires a merchant account. Merchant accounts are not all the same. Credit card companies charge different fees to process accounts. These charges vary, so shop around.

The discount rate (the amount the credit card company will deduct from each charge they process) can range from 1.5% to 5%. Some will charge transactions fees or have monthly minimums that must be met. Generally, the more automated and computerized your transactions are, the lower your discount rate will be. The discount rate can be based on the average ticket price, usually going down as the ticket price goes up. Application and setup fees (often including software and hardware to process the charges) also vary and can easily go up to $1500, so these fees must be considered when making your decision. Also, be sure to ask how soon the money will be deposited into your bank account. The deposit can be made within 24 hours or as long as seven days. Obviously, the quicker the better.

Your local bank can probably service your merchant account and will probably have reasonable rates. However, local banks are usually more conservative and may not allow as many privileges as national credit card companies. Some local banks require that the card be present and the consumer sign the charge slip, which would eliminate telephone orders or online transactions, etc. The reason for this is that a telephone order doesn't have any proof that the cardholder authorized the purchase. Telephone orders have the highest return rates and the most disputed charges, so a local bank may deny your application if you intend to do primarily phone or Internet orders.

Applying for a merchant account and getting approval is a time-consuming process. Do not make the mistake of thinking you can start in business today and get a merchant account by next week. It doesn't happen. The credit card companies require extensive documentation of your financial stability and reliability of your product and customer service. One merchant claims the applications are approved based on the weight of the information supplied. His formula for application is including everything but the kitchen sink. Not every company requires the same information, but generally they ask for product and advertising samples, and financial statements on the principals of the company as well as the company itself.

## Electronic Cash

Electronic cash is the latest development toward conducting simple and safe monetary transactions over the Internet. It is a technology which works today. Several companies supply this service and, while specifics vary, the general approach is the same. To receive payments via e-mail, download the electronic cash software onto your computer. The software is generally compatible with most types of computers. The software links you to your bank and in turn to your potential clients. Your clients will not have to be linked to your electronic cash company to pay you. When the software is running, a toolbox will appear on the screen that contains icons or buttons that if clicked will help you to make transactions with your bank and other e-cash users. Other icons when clicked will show a current status report of your account. This e-cash software, depending on the developer, can be active in the background of your graphical browser program. The e-cash software can be conveniently incorporated into the graphical browser so that the e-cash icons are visible. If the e-cash software is active in the background, it will pop up when payment is required. This e-cash software makes it easy for consumers to purchase products quickly and easily. The software is also available for UNIX users. Assuming that both your customer and his bank are equipped with the proper software and connections, they will be able to purchase with e-cash.

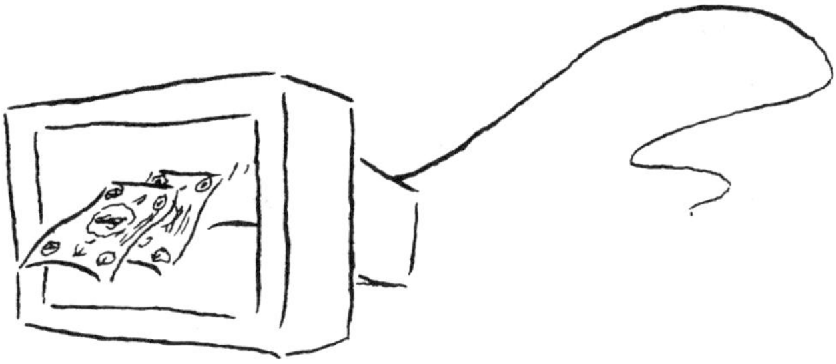

Using e-cash is similar to using an ATM (Automatic Teller Machine). The customer pulls up the e-cash computer program, and the first thing he does is verify his ownership of the account. Instead of pulling out a signed credit card, he authenticates ownership by using the icons and numbers given by the computer program. Upon a prompt, the customer requests the amount of e-cash he wants to withdraw and directs that he wishes it sent to you for payment. The software requires that he confirms the amount of e-cash, the purpose, and the payee. Then his software automatically transfers the correct value to your e-cash account. Once the cash is paid, the bank will deduct that amount from his account and your bank will add it to yours. Of course nobody ever handles the cash, but rather the software transfers the cash into the right account automatically. The best part of e-cash is that everything about the transaction is totally confidential.

How is all this made possible? Behind the scenes, the computer actually chooses the serial numbers of the electronic coins based on a random seed. The computer then hides the coins in special encryption envelopes and provides these envelopes to the ATM for a virtual signing. Once signed, the envelopes are removed from the coins leaving only the bank's validating digital signature on the serial numbers. This way, when the bank receives the coins, it cannot recognize them as coming from any particular withdrawal, because they were hidden in envelopes during withdrawal. Thus the bank cannot know when or where you shop and or what you buy. Each signed coin is unique, allowing the bank to be certain it never accepts the same coin twice. If a customer needs to identify the receipt of any of his payments he can reveal the serial number and prove that he formed it. It is important to keep a written record of the seed number chosen when the account was opened, so that if the computer breaks down, the system can recreate the coins in the account and a re-issue of the coins that were lost can be obtained. The system is designed for maximum security.

The cryptographic coding used to protect every e-cash payment is the same type of encryption that is routinely used to authenticate requests to move huge sums of money between banks. The developers of e-cash assert that the security of e-cash achieves true multiparty security: "No one (buyer, seller, bank) can cheat anyone else, no matter how they might modify their own software; even if two parties collude, they cannot cheat a third."

## Customer Support

Businesses using the Internet need to be willing to think in new ways. Successful Internet marketing is more personalized than traditional marketing. A business can't just slap up a Web site in cyberspace and hope that the big bucks will roll in. Consumers will seek out companies that respond quickly to their questions, ask for their input on products, and provide interaction with the company itself. Businesses will see themselves in alliance with their customers, creating products and services that are truly of benefit.

Internet marketing demands quick response time both for fulfillment and for answers. It also requires someone to write helpful and timely articles to keep your clientele informed. Employees who answer e-mail messages should provide a complete business name, mailing address, phone number and e-mail address.

Prepare to give excellent service. It will enhance your reputation to deliver what you have promised on time, every time. Get back to dissatisfied customers and respond to them quickly and fairly.

It's important to keep good records of your transactions. Put it in writing using e-mail. If it's a deal involving a lot of money, send a contract by regular or certified mail and ask the buyer to return a copy. For now, e-mail messages don't normally have the legal force of a signed contract.

# Section V

# Business Ideas for the Internet

## Spark Your Imagination

Are you looking for a business idea to take on the Internet? Let the following ideas spark your imagination. Read through them, keeping your own unique skills and talents in mind. Then use your creativity to establish your place in this new technological world. The ideas are divided into eight categories. The categories are not rigid, and ideas should be able to float between the divisions. The categories were established in an effort to help people who have identified different personal skills and strengths to move quickly into those areas where they will experience the greatest success. For instance, if you know you have marketing skills, you can concentrate your efforts in a marketing business. Read through all the ideas, however, because you may spot an idea from another category that you could market successfully.

# Chapter 18

## Business

For the purpose of this list, the following are ideas for businesses which require some skill or training. Obviously, because of the training involved, not every idea will work for everyone, but the ideas are presented as an catalyst for creativity. These hints should help you to generate ideas of how you can utilize your talents and skills in the Net market. For example, you would be amazed at the number of companies and professions, from lawyers to day care services, that hate to bill and do a lousy job at it. Half the time they don't follow right up with a second reminder, and it goes downhill from there. If you have accounting or business skills, you can offer to do the billing or accounting for these professionals. Start small. Find one business (doctor, plumber, pre-school, etc.) and give them a deal to get your foot in the door and gain experience. Use the Internet as a communication vehicle, so they have instant access to you. Do a good job and as your business builds, you can begin to advertise over the Net!

Tax preparation is another useful business service. It is somewhat seasonal, but if tax season is during the "slow" time of the year for your business, it could be a good way to make a little extra money. H & R Block and other commercial tax preparation services hold classes in the fall to train people as employees. Attend one of the classes, work for them for one tax season, and then start your own business. Community colleges and high school continuing education programs also have classes in tax preparation. Learn the ropes in one of these classes, then with one of the many tax preparation programs available for free on the Net, you can establish your own tax preparation business and advertise your services over the Net. Check relevant Web sites listed in the appendix for information that will keep you current on the tax law and for federal income tax forms that you can download and print. The IRS even has its own Web site, and you'll have access to documents and instructions. Your client's location is irrelevant because you can transmit the data back and forth electronically. Look in the Appendix for other sites related to tax issues.

If you possess research skills, find a way to utilize this talent. For instance, finding family roots is one of the world's most popular hobbies. If you have an interest in genealogy, you can use your Internet connection to gain access to discussion groups and research archives devoted to genealogy. These Net resources will allow you to conduct and compile records for others. People searching out their roots make the Genealogy Bulletin Board one of the most popular sites on the Net. If you have access to genealogical, census, birth, marriage, or death records, you could locate information for your clients. Many people are more than willing to pay someone to organize the information that they have collected about their ancestors.

You might have expertise in a certain area or language that would be of value. Mention your services in the appropriate newsgroups such as the *soc.genealogy* or *soc.culture* groups. Of course, there is a lot of exchange of free information in these groups; that is a good thing. People researching the same lines are more than willing to share their information. You would not be competing with that. Original research specialists charge anywhere from $10 to $25 an hour. Several programs exist that will get you started. Other helpful programs are available as shareware over the Net.

Handouts, business cards, and wedding announcements are popular items that require someone with artistic typesetting skills. Form a good relationship with a printer and hang out your shingle on the Net. Your client can view your ideas online, through e-mail or even by fax. Charge for your typesetting service and then a little extra for lining up the printer. As you begin to make money, the printer should also refer business to you. A relationship with a photographer is also important. Stay on the cutting edge. Subscribe to a graphics or typesetting publication to keep current on new ideas. One idea that hasn't hit the magazines yet is thermographic paper which changes color with temperature. When you touch a thermographic business card, it will change colors—say from red to yellow.

That catches people's attention. At least two companies in the United States will supply color-change paper to you for your clients. The paper is expensive, but well worth it.

OK, so you don't have accounting or research skills. Look through the list. Do any of these ideas appeal to you? Look over your background. Read Internet discussion group messages in areas that interest you. You may discover abilities and skills that you had not realized would be so valuable. Use your imagination! Here are just a few ideas:

Accounting
Advertising Layout
Audits
Billing and Invoicing
Business Plans
Career Planning
Claims Processing
Clothes Design
Cost Estimating
Credit Agency
Data Entry
Debugging
Electronic Circuitry Design
Energy Consultant
Fashion Merchandising
Genealogy Extraction
Hobby Supplies
Home Builder's Kit
Home Improvement Designs
Jewelry Design
Job Placement and Referral

Legal Papers
Private Investigation
Tax Consultant/Preparer
Typesetting
Video Editing

# Chapter 19

## Education

If you would like to work in education, there are many untapped areas that you can explore to form a business on the Internet. There are the traditional tutoring and manual writing opportunities. Here you share your skills and talents by training others. The training can take place either in person or through a medium such as books, cassettes or videos, but have you considered that online training is also possible through the use of IRC (Internet Relay Chat)? You could use your Internet connection to “occupy a room” and be available to answer questions, give useful information, and hear feedback from your clients. Specific and detailed answers could be sent by e-mail with or without an attached file that you have prepared offline. If you have a lot of business, and we hope you do, you can even set up an autoresponder which will answer standard questions called FAQs (Frequently Asked Questions) or send out your information packet automatically. FAQs can also be available to be downloaded by current and potential customers at your Web site. Concentrate on a unique way to market your services over the Internet.

Don't think, however, that these traditional areas are the only opportunities. Education doesn't have to necessarily involve teaching. For instance, you could form a needs-resource matching business. A good example would be in the area of scholarships. Millions of scholarship dollars are unclaimed each year. Believe it or not, applicants just don't know about the scholarships, so they never apply. Several companies have databases to match applicants' qualifications with the available scholarships, grants, or awards requiring those qualifications. The databases are large! Usually, a company maintains the database, and you just transmit the information on a client to the search company which then does the search. It should only cost you $15- $45 to have the search done, once you have established a relationship with the search company. Although at least one company has given the scholarship search programs a bad name, the service is valid, and for a very low start-up cost (several hundred dollars), you can set yourself up in the scholarship searching business. Use your computer in this business to track your own clients. You'll have an edge because you can get the information to them *fast.* Students sometimes let deadlines creep up on them and lose out on scholarship opportunities. If you can provide rush searches, and you certainly can if you communicate over the Internet, you'll have a most sought after business.

Consider ways to help your local schools. Set up a business that arranges fund-raisers for schools. Vice president Gore has told us that one goal of the present administration is to have every school and library in the country hooked up to the Internet by the year 2000. Interactive learning programs complete with graphics and sound will be in great demand throughout the country. At the present time, children can "visit" the Exploratorium in San Francisco, take a "picture tour" through the Louvre in Paris or "discover" the treasures of the Smithsonian in Washington, D.C. without leaving the classroom. Students will be learning at their own pace as they access math, science, or history programs. You could have a part in developing the next generation of problem solvers. Think of your areas of interest. Could you plan an interactive program for the computer which would teach students how to care for the planet or how to write short stories? Every field of education will need new ideas on how to teach students using the latest computer technology. You don't need to know how to write the computer program yourself; you can hire your local computer guru to do that. All you need is a good idea. Read the following list for these and other education ideas.

Abstracter
Academic Tutoring
Aptitude Testing
Article Generation
Book Lists
CD-Rom Reference
Computer Customized Education Materials
Computer Design
Computer Interactive Education Materials
Computer Tutoring
Computer Seminars

Diet Advice Newsletter
Diet Menu Planner
Disk Tutoring Programs
Fund Raising
Information Research
Internet Training
Language Learning Software
Legal Papers
Manual Writing
Music Teacher Methods
Research
Resume Preparation Advice
Retirement Planning
Scholarship Matching Service
Software Manuals
Software Programming
Speed Reading
Study Abroad Database
Support Groups
Test Scoring
Testing (all sorts)
Typing Tutor
Word Processing Classes

# Chapter 20

## Management

You would be amazed at the number of different businesses which require management help. Some of them are aware of this need, while others don't even know they need help. Think of the potential profits you can make and the service you will give if you make these businesses aware of this problem. For example, most businesses never contact their clients again once the client has dealt with them. Big mistake! A client who has already dealt with the business is the most important asset the business has. Why not keep all the client information on a computer database and "nurse" the clients along for a second sale? Have a clerk or secretary at the store or business take the names, addresses, phone numbers and other information about the clients. Enter the clients' information into the computer. This information can be sent to you electronically by e-mail or modem, and then you can help maintain a good relationship between business and customer. Once you have all of the clients' information, send them a thank-you note. Tell them about a new product or service in a letter, or send out advertising. Consider sending the clients a company newsletter or offer to coordinate the company's bill payments, handle client billing, or keep track of client services required. Your service will help the company grow.

Don't be content with just managing clients. Many companies need help managing their inventory, personnel or their budgets. Find creative ways to help companies in these areas, and your services will be invaluable. Fulfilling these services over the Net will be lightning quick. Speed is often the bottom line in today's hectic corporate world. Many company executives, for example, are required to make presentations where they need special charts, graphs, handouts, or overhead slides. The company may lack the skilled personnel, the equipment, or the time to generate these presentation materials. Yes, there are storefront commercial preparation services that will generate these materials, but they are very expensive. Without any overhead except your computer, you should be able to do a nice job preparing the needed materials if you know a graphics program inside and out. The presentations can be done in color, and they look great. No, you don't need a color printer. Local copy shops have color printers, and they will print your work for a minor charge. Graphs, charts, and even pictures can be transmitted to customers electronically.

Another way to supply management help is to contact property owners and offer to manage their property. Many of the pains of property ownership can be alleviated, or at least the pain can be reduced, by using computer programs which organize all of the functions associated with being a landlord. Many people like to own real estate, but hate to manage it, and they are willing to pay someone with a computer to keep track of all of the loose ends. (You could also offer to run utility audits for real estate owners. See ideas below on energy consultation.)

Here is a list of management ideas. Why not accept the challenge to think of other ways to render management services?

Bar Coding Services
Budgeting
Cash Flow Tracking
Client Tracking and Management
Data Management
Delivery Routes
Equipment Management
Inventory Control
Mail List Management
Manage Medical Billing, Invoicing, etc.
Mortgage Reduction Service
Newspaper Routes
Presentation Support
Property Management
Small Business Management Package
Tickler Systems
Web Site Set-up and Maintenance

# Chapter 21

## Marketing

If you become skilled in marketing, you will "hold the world by its tail." No business can succeed without marketing, and companies will pay plenty for a successful marketing campaign. Let's face it, no matter how good a product is, unless you know how to get it to the market, it is of no value. Now is the time to learn what it takes to market on the Information Superhighway. Until now, marketing and advertising have been expensive. The basis of marketing is to reach as many people as possible, and this has been very costly. The Net is an inexpensive way to discover markets. Check out the literally thousands of different newsgroups. There are groups devoted to Star Trek, pets, investments, travel, business opportunities, sports, food, software, and games. There are hundreds of interests out there. Find out what people are talking about and wish they had or wish they knew. Create a pamphlet or develop a specialized product that will be of help to those people, and you have a built-in market. Compared to traditional markets, it is not too costly to get a computer and modem and perfect your marketing skills on the Net. When you have those skills mastered, the world will literally beat a path to your door. You could also hire a computer guru to write your ads, answer inquiries and send out your catalogs or brochures by e-mail and use your time in product development, writing, or customer service. It does not matter which way you use the benefits of computer technology. You will benefit.

OK, what should you market? Well, what are your skills? If you are artistic and run a computer, for instance, consider becoming a graphic designer. Establish a relationship with a printer. There are lots of businesses that need their order forms designed or redesigned. Lots of stores use standard forms and sales receipts. If a printer will work with you (there are lots of printers looking for work, so you shouldn't have a problem finding one), you can give a store a custom form for a great price. That will help the store, the printer, and you can make money too. It is a win-win-win situation.

There's almost no risk in trying out different target markets on the Internet. Perhaps you'll find a niche market. Consider the following: in the last few years, the number of women working outside the home has jumped from 42 to 58 percent. Seventy percent of women with children under the age of six hold jobs. Time is precious for these women, and traditional store hours are inconvenient for them. They welcome alternate shopping sources that enable them to spend valuable time with their families and shop on their own schedules. They appreciate the hundreds of databases, support systems, and forums that help them keep current in their fields. These resources are available to them at very little or no cost over the Internet and are easily accessible.

Do you have a hobby or unique interest that others would like to learn? Do you throw "great" parties? Do you have a one-of-a-kind product? One woman gives kitchen parties where she lets her guests try the utensils and new recipes before they buy. She can reach suppliers and obtain out-of-the-ordinary items over the Internet. You can sell just about anything on the Net from information to hobby supplies, antiques, and office equipment. Consider the following list, or make up your own.

Astrology Advice
Antique Appraising
Baseball Cards
Birthday Party Package
Calendar of Events
Computer Art
Computer Customizing
Customized Forms
Creative Writing
Dating Idea Service
Design and Market Cross Stitch Patterns
Design and Market Cards, Labels, Banners, etc.
Direct Mail Marketing
Electronic Ad Service
Electronic Clip Art
Electronic Horoscope
Electronic Music (create and market)
Follow-up Marketing

Graphic Design
Kitchen Parties
List Brokering
Managing Stocks
Medical Billing
Newspaper Routes
Net Publishing
Party Idea Package
Personal Record Creation, Organization
Phone Consultant
Pogs
Property Management
Reunion Planning
Sales Assistance
Shopping Services
Special Occasion Announcements
Wholesale Sources
Wedding Planner

# Chapter 22

## Needs-Resource Matching

If you see a need, fill it. Computers are used in numerous fields to make a needs-resource match. For example, Dr. Norm Brown in Seattle matches companies looking for new technologies with the inventors of new technologies. His clients are actually large companies, universities, and the biggest is the federal government. He doesn't need to spend the time and the money to travel to where his clients are located because the data can be transmitted over the Internet in just minutes. He can develop an international clientele without the constraints of time and distance. Can you think of sellers, buyers, or renters that could be matched?

- Cars (you can even show pictures of them online to potential buyers)
- Real estate (pictures and descriptions of homes or property to a buyer anywhere in the world—can you

imagine the time saved by doing preselecting online before your out-of-town client arrives?)
- Recipes (low-fat, vegetarian, ethnic, grandma's Beehive cookies)
- Costumes (period costume patterns e-mailed to interested buyers, Halloween costumes for non-sewing busy mothers)

There is a demand for hundreds of match-up services.

Another good example is locating financing for new or expanding businesses. The most critical need for a new business is funding. Finding the financing for a business usually carries a good finder's fee (usually 1% - 10%). Databases of the groups that have money to invest (venture capitalists) have been put together. For a fee you can feed the information about what a business needs into a database and be matched to venture capitalists who have expressed an interest in those types of businesses.

Think of the people you know who need money for the start-up or expansion of their businesses. There are many potential clients on the Internet who are looking for venture capital. Subscribe to business mailing lists such as Internet-marketing *(listproc@einet.net* or *listserv.nervm.nerdc.ufl.edu)*. People who subscribe to these lists are interested in business topics. Some are actively searching for venture capital.

You can do two things to develop your client base. You can e-mail directly to the person, tell him about your service and let him know how he can do business with you. Or you can post a well-worded ad which tells about your business and points clients to your Web page, or at least gives them an e-mail address where they can write for more information. Yes, this is advertising, but business listservs generally don't mind your posting this sort of information if you are a member of the list. It's best to check their policy before you post.

Here are a few ideas:

Auto Parts Database Catalog
Catalog Collections
Dating Match Service
Graphic Real Estate Multiple Listing
Hobby Supplies
Period Costume Design
Seamstresses and Tailors
Referral Services
Venture Capital Funding
Volunteer Projects

# Chapter 23

## Service

Selling a service means you sell your time and/or expertise to do something for others that they either can't do or don't want to do for themselves. It makes more sense to pay someone else to do billing, track clients, or fix your refrigerator than to try to do it yourself. No, you don't need to be a highly trained technical professional. You only have to be able to provide something that others need and are willing to pay for. Recent statistics show that services now account for over half of the U.S. economy. A much larger share of the consumer budget goes for services today than for consumable products. Tony in New Jersey, for example, runs a postcard mailing service for realtors, home improvement and swimming pool contractors. He uses software to generate a highly targeted mailing list. His clients are eager for his services because he can locate new customers for them while they are working with their present clients.

Another business opportunity might be available to you in the legal field. Many lawyers make their living in collections, but you can service collections without being a lawyer. With a good program, your computer can generate the letters required to push the collections all the way to court. If the collections do go to court, you need to have a good relationship with a collection's attorney. The two of you can make a good team. Join the local credit bureau and actually put credit notations on someone's credit report. (That is often more effective than going to court.) Some states require you to be licensed, but that normally isn't a very difficult or expensive process. Several packages exist that will give you samples of letters and paperwork in line with collection laws.

If collections don't sound interesting, have you ever written a business plan, résumé, employee manual, OSHA plan, safety plan, or some other relatively complicated document? If you have, you have a skill that lots of little businesses and individuals will pay for. The computer makes changes in the basic documents easy. If you don't have experience, go to the business bulletin boards, look for categories such as Business Opportunities or subscribe to lists such as Market-L *(listproc@mailer.fsu.edu)*. Both MIT and the University of Michigan maintain resource lists for small businesses *http://cyberpreneur.umich.edu*. They can point you to programs to help small businesses. There are companies who are looking for people who can draft documents for businesses. They may even tutor you until you learn, or at least they might give you sample documents and tell you how to learn more about them.

Someone with auditing skill could set up a business auditing energy bills (gas and electric) for people and companies. In a business, it is usual to find many errors in the billings made by the gas, electric and telephone companies. The savings recovered in the audits can be very substantial. You can charge to do the audit or take a piece of the savings as your pay. With a large company an auditor sometimes makes a full year's wage in several weeks. You do have to know the rates of the utility companies, and the process takes some time to learn, but the rewards can be big.

Use your fax/modem to go into business receiving and sending faxes like a local copy center. You could also equip your computer, or charge to equip other people's computers, to receive and send e-mail to or from others. You would be amazed at how many people are afraid of technology or think they are too old or too busy to learn. These people would rather pay for this service than make the Internet connections themselves. Many businesses and homes have a computer and printer, but no Internet connection. A computer and printer can be "turned into a Net connection" for a lot less than it costs to buy a fax machine.

The number of older people in America is growing. Seniors like the convenience of shopping at home. They'd rather not have to fuss with parking or traffic, or worry about slippery roads and sidewalks. With the Internet, seniors who do not or cannot drive, who fear bad weather, or who hate public transportation won't be kept from doing their own shopping and interacting with others. They will enjoy the dignity and independence of being self-sufficient. With the Internet, declining health will not stop seniors from being able to take care of their own needs. There are so many products and services that would be of value to the seniors' market. Have you thought of maintaining a Bulletin Board System for seniors, making available electronic catalogs for online shopping, offering a wide selection of large-print books, providing tax and retirement tips in downloadable files, or planning travel arrangements and tours geared to this age?

Here are a few other service ideas:

Amortization Schedules
Billing Service
Bookkeeping Service (Contractors, Professionals, etc.)
Budgeting Service
Collection Services
Company Newsletters
Custom Calendars, Pens, etc., for Businesses
Data Entry Service
Data Conversion Service
Delivery Service
Disk Advertising Service
Disk Copying and Formatting
Document Editing
Document Design
Elderly Alert Service
Electronic Clipping Service
Energy Consultant
Family Newsletters
Fax Services
Filing Service
Fulfillment House

Genealogy Compilation
Genealogy Family Histories
Greeting Card Service
Hair Style Service
Job Location Services
Landscape Planning
Legal Filing
Legal Research
Mailing Label Addressing
Market Research
Medical Transcription
Meeting Scheduling
Menu Planning
Newsletters
Order Taking
Photographs Transferred to Computer
Postcard Mailing Service
Project Scheduling
Projecting
Record Keeping
Secretarial
Security Alert Service
Small Business Evaluation
Software Finder
Software Development
Sorting & Filing Service
Stock Market Analysis
Stock Market Investing
Survey Analysis Summary
Vacation Site Information Guide
Valuing Collectibles
Video Text Screens
Word Processing

# Chapter 24

## Computer and Technical Services

A great business can be developed operating a computer or using some other technical skill. For instance, there are thousands of people who make a nice "extra" income performing desktop publishing. Many programs are readily available to set you up as a desktop publisher. Pick one and know it inside and out. Look in the Appendix for Internet addresses of other resources. Competition is tough and making a full-time living is hard because competition can drive the price down, but it is always in demand.

Or you could use your knowledge of Internet marketing to help small businesses gain access to the power of the World Wide Web. You could start your own electronic mall and help clients develop Web sites with hypertext links. Maintaining Web sites for other businesses, large and small, will be a profitable business. The time to get in on this one is NOW. The Internet is the marketing tool of the nineties, and more and more companies are discovering that they cannot afford to ignore it if they are going to compete. They will gladly pay you to take part in this market revolution.

A computer isn't enough to get you into the polling business. However, your computer coupled with a set of 900 telephone numbers can get you started. Use one 900 line for a positive vote and one line for a negative vote. The phone companies can get a 900 line set up for you, but it will be cheaper to go to a service bureau. For a couple hundred dollars you should be able to set up two 900 lines. Get a "partner" by going to local stores, radio stations, and newspapers; pick a controversial topic and put your ad in the paper or on a radio station. You, of course, make money every time someone calls to register a vote. Share the money with your "partner." It's a great way to advertise if you do it right.

Before you or anyone buys a piece of real estate today, especially commercial real estate, the property should be scrutinized carefully. Several computer programs have been developed to accomplish the task. They take everything into account from the cost of the sewage service to the points you pay at the bank. If the analysis doesn't show the deal to be as good as the seller says it is, then you have concrete evidence to demand a lower price. If the analysis finds the deal is great—Buy! This analysis can be done for your own investments, or you can charge a price or "consulting fee" to brokers or other real estate investors. Your buyers can preselect interesting property by viewing pictures and descriptions over the Internet. Busy clients will appreciate the service, and think of how much you will save by being able to narrow down the choices before you take your buyers to a site. Travel and car expenses will go way down.

You could operate a scanning service. For this business, a scanner is required, along with the software which interfaces a computer with the scanner, but these are available for less than $1000. Businesses and individuals often have long documents that must be typed. If they are aware of your ability to scan (that is, to take type on a written page into a computer so that it can be edited and retyped), they will be happy to pay. Then you can transmit the information electronically. You should be able to scan their document faster and cheaper than they could pay someone to type the document. And remember, your clients can be anywhere in the world. One rapidly growing company develops software for computer simulations of manufacturing and health care facilities. Imagine the money companies save if they simulate the new buildings, analyze traffic flow, and make design improvements before they do any actual building. Companies are looking for ways to be more cost-effective. If you can design and implement this kind of software, your service will always be in demand.

Here are a few more ideas to get you thinking about the kind of service your business could provide.

Computer Aided Design (CAD)
Computer Design
Computer Games

Computer Graphic Arts
Computer Portraits
Computer Repair
Computer Simulations
Computer Support Service
Computer Time Rental
Create Web Sites for the Internet
Desk-top Publishing
Electronic BBS for Sales, Services or Marketing
Electronic Mail
Net Consultant
Personalized Books
Personalized Calendars
Personalized Cards
Personalized Letters
Polling
Real Estate Analysis
Scanning Services
Testing Software

# Chapter 25

## Keys for Success

We've given you a few of our ideas. You probably thought of many others as you've read through our suggestions. The keys to a successful business are:

**Decide on a product or service that you really believe in.** One man developed a pamphlet on safety when he couldn't find a ready resource. He realized that others must need the same material, too. He direct mailed it to a list available in his field of work. Now he can advertise his pamphlet over the Internet to an international clientele.

**Use what you already know**. The skills and talents that you currently have can be used to develop a business. A former buyer for a large department store decided to begin a home-based fashion consulting business so that she could stay at home near her two toddlers. She only needed a few samples to begin with, so her initial investment was minimal. She already knew her product. She loves providing a personal touch with her customers. Another advantage—she gets to buy all her own clothes at wholesale prices.

**Consider the costs, risks, and potential return**. Do research on your product and its marketability. Run test ads on the Internet. It is very inexpensive. Run an ad on a commercial online service such as America Online, Prodigy or CompuServe. People who subscribe to an online service have already demonstrated that they are willing to spend money. Your potential return is limited only by the amount of time and energy you devote to your business.

**Have pride in your work and treat people with respect and dignity**. Remember that you should choose your words carefully when you post on the bulletin boards or the Usenet newsgroups. Respond promptly to inquiries. Prepare carefully crafted answers. Work with clients to keep your product geared to their needs.

**Be aware** that there is a small extremely vocal group on the Internet who are scratching and clawing to keep it a place accessible only to the academic community and computer geeks. They are known for their rudeness, their "flaming," their unwillingness to see what is happening to the Internet as a force for positive change in the world. It should be noted that they are sometimes willing to say and do things over the Internet that they would never do if they had to see their victims face-to-face. They hide behind the anonymity of their computer screens and express exaggerated rage and "unrighteous" indignation. What they seem to have conveniently forgotten is that First Amendment rights belong to all of us, and that they will benefit also from the changes taking place. The prices of goods and services will go down; quality will go up. Con artists will be exposed before they can do much damage. The education of the next generation will be better geared to individual needs. Services that all of us want to use will be more accessible. How do you deal with this vocal few? First, ignore them. Resist the temptation to respond in kind. "Flame wars" are childish and unproductive. Second, remember that the vast majority of Internet users are honest, hardworking people like you, and they aren't offended or even annoyed at advertisements whether they are in newspapers, magazines, flyers, or posted on the Internet.

**Have a passion for what you do**. If you believe in your product and have a goal that you strongly desire to reach, you will be successful. Remember that these are not get-rich-quick schemes. Whatever effort and time you put into establishing your business will be worth it in terms of financial rewards. Moreover, if you enjoy what you are doing, your work will also be a source of tremendous personal satisfaction.

**Have a vision of the possibilities**. This is a time for creative thinking. The Internet is being shaped and rewoven every day. You can have a hand in its development. The commercial implications of this new era are incalculable, and the time is right to become involved. It takes courage and vision to recognize what is happening and to be a part of it. Of course it may seem easier to maintain the status quo, but those, who wish to be at the forefront of these rapid changes, will courageously venture forth now. You can be a part of determining the way people do business in the coming years.

# Conclusion

Realize that whether you choose to take action or not, the Information Superhighway is going to affect your life. It is the way of the future. Very soon you will find that the Internet, just like telephones and television, will be an indispensable part of civilized life. You will use it to talk to your friends, send letters, shop, get news, answer pressing questions, do research, consult experts, work with colleagues around the world, and solve problems. The Internet is here, and if you choose to become involved now, you can jump-start your future.

The Internet presents the greatest opportunity of our era. It represents a new and exciting world, and the commercial sector of this new world is poised for growth. Right now every business starting out on the Information Superhighway is starting from the same place. The playing field is level, and size or reputations are unimportant. The Internet world is so new that there are no hard and fast rules, nor are experts able to predict the future. If you enter this world, you will be a pioneer. Pioneers enter new worlds, establish the conventions, set the standards, and make names for themselves as they explore and determine what will work. Pioneers courageously set the precedents.

To decide if you can successfully pioneer this world, consider the impact computers have already had on your life and on business. The commercial world is teaming with computer use. Computers are used in almost every aspect of the business world, because they make work easier, quicker, and more precise. Those who pioneered the computer world are truly the successful entrepreneurs of our era. The Internet holds similar promise for the business world. Now is the time to recognize the promise the Internet holds for the future and resolve to become a pioneer in this new world.

A pioneer needs to be familiar with the tools to use and have the ability to creatively employ the tools in the new environment. The quickest way to learn how to use the Internet tools is to simply start playing with them. Take the plunge today. Jump in; begin to experiment with the tools of the Internet. Use your creativity to think of ways to use these tools to leverage your time and talents. The Internet is constantly changing, and so are the most effective methods for doing business over the Internet. The best way to keep abreast of the rapid changes and to utilize the incredible wealth and power of the Internet is to get on the Net and use it. Subscribe to the business lists in your areas of interest, observe what others are doing, and find your own way to do things better. Don't be afraid to examine new protocols and software and utilize all the available tools.

The opportunity to form an Internet business is knocking on the door. There are as many business opportunities as there are people and ideas. It doesn't matter what type of business you start, if you begin to explore this new market now, you will be one of the experts of the future. Perhaps the most important reason to use the Internet doesn't rest with speed, wealth, and opportunity, but with the intangible gift it will give you to leverage your time, abilities and resources, freeing you to spend your time doing the things that will enrich your life—the things that you enjoy.

Now is the time to take advantage of the wealth of opportunities for doing business over the Internet. The costs of experimenting with an Internet business are minimal. This is an excellent way to begin testing your business ideas. It doesn't matter whether it is a new business or business that is changing directions. With work, imagination, and the courage to explore this new frontier, success can be yours.

# Glossary

*Access Provider* - An organization that provides passage to the Internet.

*Anonymous FTP* - A procedure which allows the ability to retrieve the files of a remote computer that the owner has made available for access without requiring an ID or a password.

*Archie* - A tool for finding computer files that can be accessed through anonymous FTP.

*Autoresponder* - A computer system or robot that responds automatically to certain incoming e-mail requests.

*BBS (Bulletin Board System)* - An electronic posting system accessed by computer via a phone modem. Examples: Prodigy, CompuServe, and Delphi. Such forums are operated under the same concept as a bulletin board in a local supermarket; messages are posted and can be read by interested parties.

*Browser* - A hypertext interface that enables movement between WWW documents. Examples include NCSA's Mosaic, Netscape's Navigator, and Microsoft's Internet Explorer.

*Cyberspace* - A term used to describe the network world of connected computers.

*Dial-up* - A type of Internet connection. If you have a dial-up connection, you obtain indirect access to the Internet through your Internet host by modem.

*Discussion Groups* - Organized groups that focus on discussing specific topics. They can be subscribed to over the Internet.

*Domain* - An administrative organizational category of the Internet.

*Domain name* - The name given to a specific area of the Internet for organizational purposes. The domain name is that part of an Internet address that falls after the @ symbol. If the Internet or e-mail address is *ww@infodirect.com*; the domain name is *infodirect.com*.

*Download* - The process of retrieving information and transferring it to your computer files.

*E-mail* - Messages that are sent by computer to specific addresses. E-mail is short for "electronic mail."

*E-mail address* - A site which receives e-mail for a specific Internet user.

*Electronic cash* - Electronic currency available to move commerce over the Internet. It is a virtual currency having no guaranteed exchange rate.

*Encryption* - The process of encoding information so that it can be kept confidential.

*FAQs* - Frequently Asked Questions. Question/answer lists in an Internet newsgroup. FAQ's help newcomers familiarize themselves with the conventions of the newsgroup, the Internet rules, and protocols.

*Flame* - A mean or harsh Internet message, usually sent through e-mail or posted in a newsgroup.

*Freeware* - Free software available for distribution over the Internet. It can be downloaded and used without paying compensation.

*FTP* - (File Transfer Protocol) An Internet tool that allows users to retrieve a remote computer's files that the owner has made available.

*Gopher* - A menu-based Internet tool used for finding and retrieving files of all kinds.

*Graphical User Interface* - See "GUI-Graphical User Interface.

*GUI* - (Graphical User Interface) A computer program that allows the user to interface with, move about on, the World Wide Web. It operates in a visual manner using graphics to perform specific tasks.

*Home Page* - See "Web Site."

*Host* - A computer system that has a dedicated or full time connection to a network such as the Internet. It is sometimes called a node.

*Information Superhighway* - A huge computer network connecting thousands of smaller networks worldwide.

*Interface* - Gateway or format through which you and the computer communicate with one another.

*Internet* - A huge computer network connecting thousands of smaller networks worldwide.

*InterNIC* - The organization which has contracted to assign and keep track of all upper level domain names in the United States.

*IP (Internet Protocol)* - A set of technical rules and standards on the Internet for computer communication. Without protocols, computer networks could not exist, since the computers would not communicate with each other in an intelligible manner.

*Listserv* - A program that provides automatic processing of e-mail messages to mailing lists.

*Mail list* - A moderated or automatic system for transmitting e-mail messages to a group of list subscribers.

*Newsgroups* - Groups which use the Internet to make their notices available on specific topics to interested readers who subscribe.

*Newsreader* - A program which enables the user Internet access to Newsgroups Bulletin Boards.

*Net* - See "Internet."

*Netiquette* - Implied rules and customs for acceptable behavior on the Internet.

*Network* - A group of computers that are connected in a way so that they can share information.

*Path* - The route that network traffic takes from its source to its destination. Sometimes called the route.

*Posting* - A single newsgroup or listserv message.

*Protocol* - A set of technical rules and standards for computer communication. Without protocols, computer networks could not exist, since the computers would not communicate with each other in an intelligible manner.

*Server* - A computer program that provides information on the Internet. Servers respond to queries from other computers.

*Service provider* - An organization that provides passage to the Internet.

*Spamming* - The act of sending or posting the same message to as many newsgroups as possible without regard to topic of discussion.

*Storefront* - See “Web Site.”

*Telnet* - A system that allows a computer to control at least a portion of a remote computer. It is commonly used to provide off-site access to such services as automated library catalogs or Archie servers.

*Upload* - The process of transferring information from your computer to a remote computer.

*URL (Universal Resource Locator)* - An addressing system for Internet documents, including World Wide Web sites. A URL contains what type of server, where the server is located and where on that server a specific document is to be found.

*UNIX* - A computer operating system with powerful networking features. Much of the Internet has been built on a foundation of UNIX technology.

*Usenet* - The Usenet is an informal system that exchanges “news” for newsgroups.

*Veronica* - A tool for searching out Gopher-accessible information. Also an acronym for “Very Easy Rodent-Oriented Net-wide Index to Computerized Archives.”

*Web Site* - An electronic storefront on the World Wide Web that is created using HyperText Markup Language.

*White Pages* - Lists of Internet addresses accessible through the Internet.

*World Wide Web (WWW)* - The World Wide Web is a system of interconnected computer sites that are primarily linked through hypertext. Web sites can include multimedia forms, such as graphics, input fields, audio, and video.

# Appendices

# Appendix 1: Demographics and Statistics

**Web Sites:**

CERN
http://www.w3org/pub/WWW/Demographics/

GVU's WWW User Survey
http://www.cc.gatech.edu/gvu/user_surveys/User_Survey_Home.html

Hermes Project
http://www-personal.umich.edu/~sgupta/hermes/

InfoQuest Internet Surveys & Statistics
http://www.teleport.com/~tbchad/stats1.html

Internet Society
http://info.isoc.org/ftp/isoc/charts/
ftp.isoc.org

Library of Congress Internet Statistics
http://lcweb.loc.gov/global/internet/inet-stats.html

Matrix Information & Directory Services
http://www.mids.org/ids/ids.html

Netword Wizard's Internet Domain Survey
http://www.nw.com/zone/WWW/top.html

Nielsen Media Research
http://www.nielsen.com/home/media/med-res.htm

Nua
http://www.nua.ie/Choice/Surveys/SurveyMaster.html

RIPE Network Coordination Centre
http://www.ripe.net/

The Netcraft Web Server Survey
http://www.netcraft.co.uk/Survey/

Yahoo
http://www.yahoo.com/Computers/Internet/Statistics_and_Demographics

# Appendix 2: Places to Advertise on the Internet

**Search Engines:**

Banister's Submit-it
http://www.submit-it.com/

The Big Book
http://www.bigbook.com

Buy it Online
http://www.buyitonline.com

Commercial Search Engine
http://www.comcomsystems.com/search/indexadd.html

The Delphi Group
http://www.cam.org/~delphig/

Goldpages
http://goldray.com/register.sht

Marketing Database
http://www.envision.net/marketing/inet/inetdata1.html

Pagehaus
http://www.pagehaus.com

The Postmaster
http://www-netcreations.com/postmaster/doit/index.html

Selong's Submit Links Page
http://www.realitycom.com/bamboo/submit.htm

WebStep TOP 100
http://www.mmgco.com/

The World Wide Web Pavilion
http://www.catalog.com/tsw/Pavilion

wURLd Presence™
http://www.ogi.com/wurld/

**Classified Ads:**

Access Market Square
http://webtrade.com

American Business Classifieds
http://www.webcom.com/abc/forsub1.html

Entrepreneur Net
http://cyberzine.org/html/Entrepreneur/enetpage2.html

Epages (Only accepts non-commercial ads)
http://ep.com

The Exchange (Idaho and Washington)
http://www.iea/~adlinkex

The Inter.net
http://www.nauticom.net/www/future21/class.html

Internet Marketing Report
http://www.mbs.program.com/MBS/index2.html

Internet Resources Database
http://www.mbmarktcons.com/mbmarkt/cl-phpag.htm

Ultimate Solutions
http://www.ultimate.org/classifieds

The Weekly Bookmark and WBAds Homepage
http://www.webcom.com/weekly/wbads.html

**Announcements:**

Net-Happenings
NET-HAPPENINGS@LISTS.INTERNIC.NET

New World Marketing
Send an e-mail message to:
scotta@nuworld.com
Subject:
category of announcement such as BOOK, AD, WEB SITE, etc.
Message in body:
a short description of your product, service or site.

# Appendix 3: Business and Marketing Listservs

The List of Marketing Lists
http://nsns.com/MouseTracks/tloml.html

Autoshoppers
Send email message to:
autoshoppers@han1.hannah.com
Subject:
subscribe

Applied Global Marketing
Send an email message to:
listserv@ukcc.uky.edu
Message in body:
subscribe globmkt *your name*
Reply with a confirmation message “ok” within 48 hours

Imall-L
Send an email message to:
listserv@netcom.com
Message in body:
subscribe Imall-L *your email address*

Internet-Marketing
Send an email message to:
im-sub@i-m.com
No message is required

Internet Sales

Send an email message to:

is-sub@mmgco.com

No message is required

Market-L

Send email message to:

listproc@mailer.fsu.edu

Message in body:

subscribe Market-L *yourname*

You will receive a confirmation number. You then reply with a password of your choice.

Market Segmentation Discussion List

Send an email message to:

maiser@mail.telmar.com

Message in body:

subscribe Mktseg

Marketing with Technology

Send an email message to:

listserv@uhccvm.uhcc.hawaii.edu

Message in body:

subscribe MT-L *your name*

Reply with a confirmation message "ok" within 48 hours

NetMarket-L, etc.

Send an email message to:

listserv@Citadel.Net

Message in body:

subscribe NetMarket-L subscribe info4U-L

subscribe HomeBased-L

# Appendix 4: Keeping Informed

**Web Sites:**

IdeasDigest™

http://www.ideas.wis.net/

Inter-Links

http://www.nova.edu/Inter-Links/

InterNIC Net Happenings

http://www.mid.net/NET/

Send an email message to:

listserv@lists.internic.net

Message in body:

subscribe net-happenings *yourname*

Media Central

http://www.mediacentral.com/info/Join/join-now.html

Savetz's Unofficial Internet Public Domain Index

http://www.northcoast.com/savetz/pd/pd.html

**Miscellaneous:**

Yanoff's Internet Services List

ftp ftp.csd.uwm.edu/pub

Web Marketing Today Newsletter

Send an email message to:

listserv@wilsonweb.com

Message in body:

subscribe web-marketing

# Appendix 5: FTP Sites

rtfm.mit.edu

ftp archive.umich.edu

sumex-aim.stanford.edu

ftp oak.oakland.edu

ftp ftp.sura.net

ftp quartz.rutgers.edu

ftp wuarchive.wustl.edu

# Appendix 6: Bulletin Board Systems

**Web Sites:**

Richard Mark's Select BBSs on the Internet
http://dkeep.com/sbi.htm

Home Office Business Exchange
modem 519-633-6574

Sonie's Creations BBS
modem 416-533-4471

Strictly Business! BBS
199.3.12.13

Data Connection
modem 909-698-7257

SoftFind
modem 904-323-1910

Online Network
http://coral-springs.info-access.com/OnLine/

Metropolis™ Systems BBS Complex
http://www.metro.bbs.com/metcom.htm

The File Bank
http://www.tfb.com/
telnet bbs tfb.com

# Appendix 7: Accounting

**Web Sites:**

Accountant's Home Page (An Index to finance-related sites on the Web. Many links to government resources.)
http://www.servtech.com/re/acct.html

Accounting Resources
http://www.lib.lsu.edu/bus/account.html

ANet—International Accounting Network
http://www.scu.edu.au/ANetHomePage.html

AuditNet (Audit/Accounting/Finance email directory)
http://www.cowan.edu.au/mar/home.htm

accounting.org (Lists and links to major accounting sites on the Internet.)
http://www.accounting.org/

FinanceNet (Listings of Government Asset Sales, libraries, mailing lists, discussion forums, and other resources.)
http://www.financenet.gov/

# Appendix 8: Asset Protection and Taxes

**Web Sites:**

ABA Tax Section
http://grover.abanet.org/tax/sites.html

US Copyright Forms
http://lcweb.loc.gov/copyright/forms.html

Copyright Information
http://www.cyberhighway.net/~alnor/index.html

Copyright laws and FAQs
ftp rtfm.mit.edu/pub/usenet-by-group/news.answers/ law/copyright/faq

CHI, Research Inc. (Patent searching)
http://www.chiresearch.com

LegaLees™ (Asset protection and licensing)
http://legalees.com/

The Legal Information Institute
http://www.law.cornell.edu/topical.html

The Legal List
http://www.lcp.com/The-Legal-List/TLL-home.html

JohnSon's Tax Page
http://www.unf.edu/students/jmayer/tax.html

US Tax Code Online
http://www.fourmilab.ch/ustax/ustax.html

Frank McNeil's Income Tax Information
http://www2.best.com/~ftmexpat/html/taxsites.html

TaxWeb
http://www.taxweb.com/

IRS
http://www.irs.ustreas.gov/prod/cover.html

**Mailing list:**

Send e-mail message to:
*lasser@acc.fau.edu*
Message in body:
subscribe ATTAX-L

**Usenet Newsgroup:**

misc.taxes

# Appendix 9: Dietetics and Nutrition

**Web Sites:**

The Cyberkitchen™
http://www.jbot.com/cyberkitchen

Ask the Dietitian by Joanne Larsen, M.S., R.D.
http://www.hoptechno.com/rdindex.htm

The National Association of GCRC Research Dietitians
http://crcdec.swmed.edu/~nagrd/

International Food Information Council (also has a mailing list)
http://ificinfo.health.org/

Vegetarian Resource Group (Many articles of interest on school lunch, diabetes, recipes, etc.)
http://envirolink.org/arrs/VRG/

NIDDK
http://www.niddk.nih.gov

National Institutes of Health
http://www.nih.gov

Trans Fat InfoWeb
http://204.252.76.40/0001t1a.html

FatFree: The Low Fat Vegetarian Archive
http://www.fatfree.com/
ftp ftp.geod.emr.ca/pub/Vegetarian/Recipes/FatFree

The FoodWeb (An encyclopedia of food from the earth)
http://www.fatfree.com/foodweb/

USDA Nutrient Values (A searchable index of the USDA database)
http://www.fatfree.com/usda/

16th International Congress of Nutrition
http://www.nrc.ca/confserv/iuns97/welcome.html

Department of Food Science & Nutrition, University of Minnesota
http://fscn1.fsci.umn.edu/

The Virtual Nutrition Center
http://www-sci.lib.uci.edu/~martindale/
Nutrition.html

Institute of Food Science & Technology
http://www.easynet.co.uk/ifst/ifsthp3.htm

NutriGenie
http://users.aol.com/nutrisoft/ngmd40.html

Nutrisoft On-Line
http://www.microserve.net/~cyberloc/pn.html

Institute of Food Research
http://www.ifrn.bbsrc.ac.uk/

Explore Food Engineering with R. Paul Singh
http://nachos.engr.ucdavis.edu/~rpsingh/index.html

Center for Food Safety and Applied Nutrition
http://vm.cfsan.fda.gov/list.html

Functional Foods for Health
http://www.ag.uiuc.edu/~ffh/ffh.html

FDA
gopher:// zeus.esusda.gov
http://www.fda.gov/bbs/
telnet www.fda.gov

**Mailing Lists:**

food-comp. Food composition issues and data.
Send e-mail message to:
list-owner@INFOODS.UNU.EDU
Message in body:
subscribe food-comp *your name*

food-eng. Discussion and announcements on food engineering topics.
Send e-mail message to:
owner-foodeng@ucdavis.edu
Message in body:
subscribe food-eng *your name*

food-for-thought. Discussion on all aspects of food.

Send email message to:

mailbase@mailbase.ac.uk

Message in body:

subscribe food-for-thought *your name*

foodlink. Food safety issues.

Send e-mail message to:

owner-foodlink@listproc.wsu.edu

Message in body:

subscribe foodlink *your name*

IFT. Institute of Food Technologists Food Science Communicators

Send e-mail message to:

listserver@lists.acs.ohio-state.edu

Message in body:

subscribe IFT *your name*

NUTEPI. This list deals with nutritional epidemiology.

Send e-mail message to:

LISTSERV@TUBVM.CS.TU-BERLIN.DE

Message in body:

subscribe NUTEPI *your name*

Nutrition Resources Bulletin

Send email message to:

majordomo@sfu.ca

Message in body:

subscribe nutrition-resbul

end

**Newsgroups:**

sci.med.nutrition

alt.food

alt.food.low-fat

alt.food.fat-free

alt.support.diet

alt.med.allergy

alt.food.professionals

alt.support.eating-disord

misc.health.diabetes

alt.recovery.compulsive-eat

alt.creative.cooking

# Appendix 10: Business

**Web Sites:**

Business Resource Center
http://www.kcilink.com/brc/

Council of Better Business Bureaus
http://www.bbb.org/

Federal Trade Commission
http://www.ftc.gov/

Nijenrode Business Resources
gopher://zeus.nijenrode.nl:70/11/Business

Open Market's Commercial Sites Index
http://www.directory.net

Project 2000 A Research Program on Marketing in Computer-mediated Environments
http://www2000.ogsm.vanderbilt.edu/eli.cgi/

A Cyberpreneur's Guide to the Internet
http://asa.ugl.lib.umich.edu/chdocs/cyberpreneur/Cyber.html

Economic BBS
telnet ebb.stat-usa.gov
gopher:// una.hh.lib.umich.edu:70/11/ebb

Entrepreneur Information Guide
http://www.magpage.com/~rispoli

Entrepreneurs on the Web
http://sashimi.wwa.com/~notime/eotw/EOTW.html

IndustryNet
http://www.industry.net/

Small Business Administration
gopher://www.sbaonline.sba.gov/

Wimsey Corporation
http://www.wimsey.com

Market Link
http://www.m-link.com/

**Newsgroups:**

alt.business

alt.business.hospitality

alt.business.insurance

alt.business.import-export

alt.business.misc

alt.business.multi-level

alt.forsale

biz.general

biz.jobs.offered

biz.marketplace.discussion

biz.marketplace.international

biz.marketplace.noncomputer

biz.misc

misc.business.consulting

misc.consumers

misc.business.facilitators

misc.entrepreneurs

misc.entrepreneurs.moderated

misc.forsale.non-computer

misc.wanted

misc.invest

rec.antiques.marketplace

rec.arts.book.marketplace

rec.audio.marketplace

rec.autos.marketplace

rec.bicycles.marketplace

rec.crafts.marketplace

rec.photo.marketplace

rec.skiing.marketplace

rec.travel.marketplace

# Appendix 11: Resources for Web Site Creation

**Web Sites:**

Background Images Archive
http://www.psy.uwa.edu.au/bkgs/bkg_menu.htm

Bumpy: The Land of Textures
http://www.primenet.com/~piglett/textures.html

Excavations: DiP
http://www.algonet.se/~dip

Free Web Graphics by Pam Bytes
http://www.tgn.net/~pambytes

Freebies
http://www.tripod.com/~tabbie/index.html

Home Page Toolbox for Mac
http://www.foxnet.net/users/apeltonen/toolbox.html

HTML Style Guide & Test Suite
http://www.charm.net/~lejeune/styles.html

Iconolog96
http://www.ozemail.com.au/~afactor/iconolog.html

Iconomics (Thousands of design quality clip art images)
http://www.iconomics.com

Illusionist's Art Gallery
http://www.infohaus.com/access/by-seller/Illusionist/HIDDEN.artpage.free.html

Center for Advanced Instructional Media
http://info.med.yale.edu/caim/StyleManual_Top.HTML

Internet Desktop Publishing Jumplist
http://www.cs.purdue.edu/homes/gwp/dtp/dtp.html

The comp.fonts Home Page
http://jasper.ora.com:80/comp.fonts/index.html

The Scanning FAQ
http://www.dopig.uab.edu/dopigpages/FAQ/The-Scan-FAQ.html

Barry's Clip Art Server
http://www4.clever.net/graphics/clip_art/clipart.html

Tim Walker's New HTML Virtual Tutor (Good place for backgrounds, icons, and more)
http://www.netins.net/showcase/walker/html/index.html

Timid Textures
http://www.santarosa.edu/~tmurphy/texture.html

The Transparent Interlaced GIF Resource Page
http://dragon-jpl.nasa.gov/~adam/transparent.html

WebAID
http://webaid.com

**Newsgroups:**

alt.aldous.pagemaker

# Index

# Index

## A



## B



## C



## D

## E



## F



## G



## H

## I



## L



## M



## N



## P



## R

## S



## T



## U



## V



## W